DOING BETTER THAN YOUR BEST

Recreating Your World through Academic Excellence...

Excel Ogugbue, PhD.

Copyright © 2014 Excel Ogugbue

First Edition

All rights reserved.

DBTB Books, Richmond, TX 77407-4062

Learn more about DBTB Books or contact us by visiting our Facebook page at https://www.facebook.com/DBTBbooks

No part of this publication may be reproduced, stored in a retrieval system or transmitted in any form or by any means, electronic, mechanical, photocopying, recording, scanning or otherwise, except under the terms of the Copyright, Designs and Patents Act 1988 or under the terms of a license issued by the Copyright Licensing Agency Ltd.

ISBN-13: 9780991290628

Library of Congress Control Number: 2013958430

Book Cover & Design by PIXEL eMarketing INC.

Legal Disclaimer

The publisher and the author make no representations or warranties with respect to the accuracy or completeness of the contents of this work and specifically disclaim all warranties, including without limitation warranties for a particular purpose. No warranty may be created or extended by sales or promotional materials. The advice and strategies contained herein may not be suitable for every situation.

Neither the publisher nor the author shall be liable for damages arising herefrom. The fact that an organization or website is referred to in this work as a citation and/or a potential source of further information does not mean that the author or the publisher endorses the information the organization or website may provide or recommendations it may make.

Further, readers should be aware that Internet websites listed in this work may have changed or disappeared between when this work was written and when it is read.

This book is dedicated to:

My deceased father and
my foundation, Chibuike D. Ogugbue.

and

My mother, Elizabeth N. Ogugbue,
who sacrificed her life to ensure that
my siblings and I became college graduates.

Acknowledgements

I wish to express my deepest appreciation to my mother, *Elizabeth N. Ogugbue*, for always being there for me with constant support and encouragement, and to my siblings, *Kelechi, Chiemela, Chinanu, Ugochi,* and *Chinomso*. Without you, my story would never be complete, and you remain my inspiration to never compromise in integrity and to be the best I can be.

To my sister in law, *Miriam*, for her infusion of energy to get this book done. Thanks for all your support and prayers.

To all my friends, who have loved, supported, and prayed for me along the way.

My love and thanks to everyone who has been a part of my world and who has contributed to my becoming who I am today. I could not have made it this far without you all. These include the many great authors and speakers whose books and audio messages have helped shape my life. With every life that is touched through this book, you share the credit.

A big thank you to my editor *Melissa Se* and her team for their creativity and attention to detail in designing the cover page and editing and proofreading this book. Thank you for helping me utilize the printed page in order to inspire people with my story.

Finally, huge thanks to all of you who are reading. I want to also acknowledge your support as you help spread this message of hope to your family and friends. Thank you very much.

Contents

Introduction 1
Chapter 1: Days Of My Life 9
Chapter 2: Becoming a Businessman 17
Chapter 3: My Academic Pursuit of Excellence 25
Chapter 4: Getting University Admission 37
Chapter 5: Preparing for Exams 43
Chapter 6: The Smart Student's Credo 51
Chapter 7: Shaping Young Minds 57
Chapter 8: Exceeding Expectations 69
Chapter 9: PetroBowl Champions 79
Chapter 10: Money Matters 93
Chapter 11: Do Right 117
Chapter 12: The Gift of Life 123
Chapter 13: The Higher Life 131
Chapter 14: Living My Dream 149
Chapter 15: No More Excuses 157
Chapter 16: Never Give Up 167
Chapter 17: Nothing Just Happens 175
Closing Words: See the Big Picture 197

Introduction

My parents named me Chinenye Ogugbue back in 1980 when I was born in Nigeria, but ever since college, my friends have called me Excel, which is my middle name. Growing up in a Christian home as an active believer, I was introduced to divine foundations and principles for success. Determined to become successful, I have applied these principles to my life over the years, and by God's grace, I have attained exceptional heights in my academic life and have a promising career as a petroleum engineer in the oil and gas industry. I am grateful to have left where I used to be, and I have a resolve to continue in this winning lane of life as I work towards the fulfillment of my divine purpose. Through academic seminars, teaching in schools, volunteer tutoring, and youth programs, I have encouraged people to overcome adversity by sharing my unique story on the rewards of faith, focus, diligence, honesty, love, and self-discipline.

There were a lot of obstacles to overcome along my way to the good life, including growing up with my five siblings and my mum after losing my dad to a ghastly motor accident as a young student. My mother convinced me that I could recreate my world through academic excellence. I could become great and have a better life if I did well in school. Pure determination in the face of inadequate resources pulled me through college, where I graduated with honors and got a scholarship to further my education in the United States. In this book, I share with you my experiences in dealing with adversity and obstacles, some of them unique to growing up as a poor kid in Nigeria. I believe the secrets to every success (personal, academic, and career) that I have achieved to date are in my personal stories. The sharing of our learning is what connects us to each other; a responsibility humans carry for being human. I hope that you will enjoy and learn from my story.

After telling my story to someone one day, I realized that my study habits and approach to life in general, which came so easily to me, could be taught to others and, more importantly, needed to be taught to others. So I looked carefully at the ways successful people go about their lives and began to compare them with my own attitudes to life. What I realized is that people must go the extra mile to achieve extraordinary results. For me, these include my experiences raising money to fund my education and to support my family and my study habits as well as inspiring stories of academic excellence, honesty, and integrity. Hence, this book is filled with inspiring case histories and delivers a powerful message about working towards achieving your goals, staying focused, and seeing the big picture.

Sometimes I have wondered what sets apart people who achieve from those that do not achieve. As we strive to better ourselves and achieve our goals, it can be frustrating at times to watch other people enjoying life as we and others around us struggle. Is it luck? Influence? Fate? Are these high fliers just more astute than the rest of us? While all these attributes may play a role for the outliers, I strongly believe there are other qualities that are more telling when it comes to deciphering what it takes to attain tremendous success in life. What is wrong with me? All of us seem to have this thought that there is something wrong with wanting to achieve, to be different than those around us. Why am I like this? We ponder this question as we watch those around us simply get by. We have all asked ourselves these questions at one time or another. We wonder why we are motivated to be more when we look around and see so many settling for simply being less than their best. Behind these perplexing questions lies the root question that so many of us face: "Is it possible for someone with my background, my educational level, my personality, my family history, my age, or my technical skills to obtain success?"

The answer to this question is a definite YES! Your success is not and cannot be determined by what you currently have or your place in life right now, but your choice must be to have your life be determined by what you do with what you have. As you do, you will get to realize the fact that at the end, what really matters are the lives you touch along the way and how you finish your journey. Hence, successful individuals look beyond their circumstances to their possibilities.

Success requires planning and hard work. Great success is recorded in diligent pursuits. Diligence involves investing your abilities, your strength, your desire, and all you have into the pursuit of your mission. I often hear people say, "What's meant to be will be," but that is only true after you have completed your part. I belong to the camp where people believe that nothing just happens; your decisions and choices in life are what create your reality. The truth is, until you understand the process that leads to your success, you will either delay or forfeit the fulfilled and happy life that is possible.

As you read this book, you will discover new ideas and new ways of doing better. You will feel that you can do better, and there will be a genuine desperation to discover what to do and how to go about getting to your next level. If you do, it is for you and for those like you that this book is written. Most importantly, as you read this book, you are going to develop a hunger to always do better than your best. As a result of my passion for sharing knowledge and insights that will help people achieve their goals, dreams, and aspirations, this book will challenge and motivate you to do more, and accomplish more, in every aspect of your life. This book is written for ambitious people who are determined to change their life, achieve more in life, and accomplish well above average; people who want to achieve everything that is possible for them in life.

By reading *Doing Better Than Your Best,* you will discover the habits, knowledge, traits, and principles that are necessary for academic and career success. Doing better than your best takes away the guilt of "I could have done better." It makes for a happier, successful life because you consistently live up to your standards, or you are possibly exceeding them. Doing better than your best is a call towards a lifestyle that makes you compete with yourself and not with others because you are consistently living with genuine passion for an unwavering pursuit of excellence, striving for a track record of high performance, and fulfilling your divine purpose. You may ask, how is this possible?

In his book, *Better Than Good: Creating a Life You Can't Wait to Live,* Zig Ziglar listed the following 15 ways as a tool you could use to measure your status on doing better than good.[1] You are doing better than good when you…

- …clearly understand that failure is an event, not a person; that yesterday ended last night; and today is your brand new day.
- …have made friends with your past, are focused on the present, and are optimistic about your future.
- …know that success (a win) does not make you and failure (a loss) does not break you.
- …are filled with faith, hope and love and live without anger, greed, guilt, envy, or thoughts of revenge.
- …are mature enough to delay gratification and shift your focus

---

[1] Ziglar, Zig. Better Than Good. Thomas Nelson, Inc. (2006)

from your rights to your responsibilities.
- …know that failure to stand for what is morally right is the prelude to being the victim of what is criminally wrong.
- …are secure in who you are so you are at peace with God and in fellowship with man.
- …have made friends of your adversaries and have gained the love and respect of those who know you best.
- …understand that others can give you pleasure, but genuine happiness comes when you do things for others.
- …are pleasant to the grouch, courteous to the rude, and generous to the needy.
- …love the unlovable and give hope to the hopeless, friendship to the friendless, and encouragement to the discouraged.
- …can look back in forgiveness, forward in hope, down in compassion, and up with gratitude.
- …know that "he who would be the greatest among you must become the servant of all."
- …recognize, confess, develop, and use your God-given physical, mental, and spiritual abilities to the glory of God and for the benefit of mankind.
- …stand in front of the Creator of the universe and He says to you, "Well done, thou good and faithful servant."

The personal stories shared in *Doing Better Than Your Best* bolster, embolden, and encompass these ideas. I believe they will motivate you because in writing this book, I have connected some dots between events in my life that had been a great source of motivation for me. And I want you to connect those same dots in your life. As you do, you will draw insights from my story on how to accomplish more than you ever dreamed possible, and you will discover what it takes to do better than your best and rise above fear and failure to embrace the quality of life you are meant to have.

Please join me as I share this unforgettable journey that God took me through to discover what it takes to perform at levels much higher than one can attain by mere efforts. Along the way, we will learn what the winning attitude, "Doing Better Than Your Best," is all about. I have attempted to share these excerpts from my life as candidly as possible. And by the way, when it matters, some places and people's names have been changed and physical descriptions altered to protect certain individuals' privacy. This book is the story of how I bought into my mother's advice and decided to put in better than my best efforts to make sure that I achieved set goals. It is about my attitude towards my education, God, life, work, and money; what I did; how I raised money to help fund my education; how I studied; how I learned from my failures and successes; when I performed below expectations, how I reacted; what I did to make it to the top; what I did to stay at the top; How I got my priorities right, and how I praised God and remained thankful for all the breakthroughs he wrought in my life.

The chapters that follow explain my story and my life journey so far. I hope it motivates and inspires you. At just 16 years old, Olympic gymnast and gold medalist Gabby Douglas had accomplished a lot, and she told her story in a memoir titled *Grace, Gold and Glory: My Leap of Faith*. Upon her book's acquisition by Zondervan Publishing Company, Gabby stated[2]: *"Even before I competed in the Olympics, I always wanted to write a book. Of course, there'll be a lot of stories about gymnastics, but the book will also be about how much my family and I have overcome during our journey."* She said she hopes her story will become an inspiration to others. *"I want people to read my story and say, 'If Gabby can do it, I can do it, too. Anything is possible."*

That is an experience I want people to get from reading *Doing Better Than Your Best*. If Excel can make it, despite all odds, I can

---

2 Zondervan Acquires Two Books by U.S. Olympic Gold Medalist Gabby Douglas http://www.prweb.com/releases/2012/9/prweb9875165.htm

make it too. Anything is possible. If God can do it for me, He can do it for you too. The Bible says[3] that God raises the poor from the dust and lifts the needy from the ash heap that He may place them among princes. I so believed in this scripture because I knew poverty. I touched it with my hands; I felt it growing up. I lived it and smelled it, but I never allowed it to steal my joy. I was content with what I had, and no one ever knew when I had no money for breakfast, lunch, or dinner. Today my story has changed. Going forward, I am so sure about tomorrow because I know the principles traded to get me where I am today, and here, I commit to paper the winning ways that helped me move from grass to grace. Let me add that there is nothing magical about the knowledge you will acquire through this book; it is a practical engagement of tested and proven principles.[4] I am a living witness—the good news is the same could become your story, if you understand and play your part.

It all starts with learning, understanding, and loving the winning attitude, *doing better than your best*. Read on and enjoy!

---

3 See Psalm 113:7–8
4 Oyedepo, David. Exploring the secrets of success, Dominion Publishing House, 1998

Chapter 01

Days Of My Life

Some days in life are difficult to forget. It may be because we relive them over and over again and they show up in our minds without reason or knowing why they have been brought to the forefront. Suddenly, a memory appears. Maybe it was triggered by an event that just occurred. Who knows? They just appear, in all their strength and force. They are too strong to be replaced by other, happier times even after we have moved past them. The emotions are so strong that they keep churning to the top and demanding our attention.

Perhaps these memories, especially those from our childhood, have seared our soul in some deep and ever-changing way. All I really know about these memories is that each time we do relive them, we learn just a little bit more about ourselves by looking at the arc of our life. And that never really gets old. As long as we take breaths, there is more to learn about whom we are and why we are here. Learning is the purpose of life; the reason each of us is given different abilities to help us make our way in life. The sharing of our learning is what connects us to each other and is a responsibility humans carry for being human. And maybe there is something you can learn from my life, if I am willing to feel these memories and write about them.

This is a difficult thing to do. But I will start my story long ago, with a day that started out as a day that seemed much like any other day to a boy like me, one who would be turning eight in just 55 days. On that day, at the beginning of the vicious 'mber[5] months in Nigeria, my mother, my five siblings, and I waited all day, all night, and then some, worry increasing by sun setting and then dawning again, for the return of my mother's cherished husband and our loving father. We did not know as we waited that he would not return to us once more but be lost forever.

At the time, my father, who was the dean of studies for St. Anne's Secondary School Umuobasi Amavo, had travelled by public transportation to Owerri to process a number of examination registration materials for his college students. On his way back, the car he boarded had a flat tire; the driver lost control, and the rest of the story's details are beyond me. They are details that only those that were there can know for sure. But what we do know and what we scraped together from others is that the car was a 504 Wagon Peugeot and had too many passengers, which may have contributed to the tire going flat. When that happened, my dad was sitting at the back row seat with two other passengers. Even now, we only know that he sustained a massive head injury, one that caused immense and immediate damage, and he was pronounced dead by the time the emergency ambulance could get him to the hospital, which was such a long ways away.

We have heard that other passengers, interviewed not long after the accident, confessed that he was advising the driver not to touch the brakes; he knew what would happen if the driver tried to apply

---

5   'mber months refer to the months of the year from September to December—most road accidents happen around 'mber months as people travel for holidays.

the brakes to a car that had lost a tire with a flat. The story is told that the car tumbled several times and entered the bush, where it settled in a silent homage to the pain the accident caused and to the life that was lost in a moment. I can only imagine the state of his mind while the car was somersaulting over and over again. I can only imagine what his thoughts were as he breathed his last breath of fresh air. I imagine he fought to stay alive, refusing to take that last breath, knowing that he had a caring wife and six loving children awaiting his return, depending on him for their welfare.

As much as I see that day as one of my toughest days to endure and a turning point in my life, I strongly believe that it must have been a tougher day for him. They say these moments slow down dramatically, and if this is so, he must have had time to wonder how we could get by without him, moments to worry about his children's future without a father. Though my dad did not own any personal car, I could not help but ask myself: "Instead of travelling by public transportation, could things have turned out different if my dad was driving his own car on that fateful day? What would our life have been if dad had survived the vehicle accident on that day?" Assuredly, he would have been there to care for our welfare and later help us make important career and life decisions. But really, to have someone who desires the best for their children, who demands the future be the best it can, is what a child really needs. And, as you see, we still had our mother. We still had that one parent to guide us.

The following day was the beginning of a new era for me. It was the beginning of my life without my father. My father was charismatic and had a warm heart. He was gentle; he was not the kind of father who would lay down the law by speaking harshly to his children. In retrospect, I could envisage my mother in her teary eyes looking up and asking God, *"Why?"* and entreating, *"Oh Lord, how can we get by without Daddy?"*

The future looked gloomy. How, we wondered, is my mother going to take care of six children with her associate degree in education and her marginal salary as a public school teacher? Where do we go from here? What will happen to us? How will we eat or pay the rent?

At that time, the social norm was for uncles and aunts of the children to choose who amongst the fatherless kids they could bring in to join their family. They could train the child and teach them a trade so the child could contribute and find a way to make a living. Despite the fact that one of my uncles was the incumbent Imo State commissioner for commerce and industry when my father died and several uncles were successful businessmen in different cities, I cannot recall if it was that none of my relatives offered to be of help to us or if my mum deliberately chose not to accept any of the six of us being sent to live with them. Somehow and for some reason, we stayed together.

Nonetheless, mother managed to bring a sense of harmony and security to our seven member family. We were forced into relocating from our cozy, three-bedroom, single-family home to a 12-ft by 10-ft single room in the city; a single room for a mother and her six kids. We were in dire straits, and our mother was doing the best she could in facing this new life.

I remember all too well these days of our humble beginnings—the beginning of our days as a family without a father. I remember the meeting we had in our single room "home" when my mother told us of her dream, a grand dream to make sure that every one of us would become a college graduate. How this was going to happen, she had no idea. Neither did I, but she did promise that with trust in God and by all of us living in harmony and within our means, we would move through the difficult times to a better future.

As a first step, she found a cleaning job for one of my brothers, Chiemela, in a reputable bank. A simple and humble job to be sure, but her thoughts were that this kind of an environment would offer my brother the benefit of seeing the importance of education. There, in the bank, even working as a cleaning person, my brother would see those that were successful and model himself after them. He would see how these successful people acted, spoke, and lived. He would desire to achieve that life. This kind of an environment could help anyone understand the importance of education. It certainly did for my brother. As I am writing this story, Chiemela is a top-ranking employee in a reputable financial institution in Nigeria. But while my brother was waiting to gain admission into the university, he spent most of his spare time hanging out with auto technicians. My mother cried when my brother would spend his time hanging out at the mechanic's shop with technicians. Mother's fear was that he would lose the motivation that he needed to make it through college because by associating with those who had not made it through high school, he would feel that this was a "good enough" life. He would feel there was no need to be more than a simple technician, and my mother's dream for her children would go unfulfilled.

This thinking is so true. It supports the wise saying that the company you keep can determine how far you go in life. Perhaps it is the most fundamental rule of life. We cannot become what we do not see as possible. And we cannot see what is possible if we are not around these role models. This, as my mother knew, determines whether you will become a trained professional or a roadside mechanic. It will determine the kind of opportunities that could come your way. My mother knew that we could improve our lives, but she knew that we could only improve our lives if we chose to travel as the same kind of people that successful people would want to be around.

"We are going to live within our means, we are going to live truthfully, we are going to depend on each other, we are going to live an honest life, we are…if that means eating once in a day or fasting when you're not supposed to, we are going to do it," said Mother, making us understand the power of education. She explained how it is better to spend four or more years in college to build the qualifications to become a professional than to spend the time learning through apprenticeship or learning a roadside trade, which usually comes at lower cost to the parents but does not give the children the life a mother wants for her children.

Because of her teachings and her telling us that if we sacrificed the temporary, we could have the forever, today I can go to Walmart Superstore, buy five ears of corn, peel them, boil them to my taste, and eat them all as if I am enjoying some snacks while watching a movie. But as a teenager, these five ears of corn served as lunch or dinner for a family of seven. The lean times, the hard times, and the times of believing what my mother told us have brought me the "today" that I so desired and worked for so hard.

In retrospect, I cannot even imagine how we survived, but one thing I know is that we believed in Mum's message. There were many unknowns, but we kept our hands clean, lived within our means, and refused to be bothered by what we did not have. *"If you must have something, make sure it's something that will take you towards the future that you want in five years' time or ten years' time or life after college,"* Mum would always advise. It was easy for me to make the choice to follow my mother's advice because I wanted to end up like Dr Ben Carson, who wrote the book *Gifted Hands*[6], or Chike in *Chike and the River*[7] by Chinua Achebe, or Eze in the book *"Eze Goes to School"*[8] written by Onuora Nzekwu, or so many others, who began in difficult circumstances but believed in a life that would be a better one. In addition to the Bible, these were the books that helped shape my thoughts in my childhood and motivated and sustained me.

To be honest, even as kids, we did not see how our mum was going to be able to send six of us to the university, but we believed in God. And today, I would like to tell you that her dreams have been achieved. We all have at least a college diploma to our credits, and even beyond a college diploma, two of my siblings have already completed post-graduate degrees (Masters) in their respective fields of study; I have already earned my doctorate degree in Petroleum Engineering from the University of Oklahoma Norman in the United States.

---

6   Carson, Ben. Gifted Hands. Zondervan (1990)
7   Achebe, Chinua. Chike and the River. Cambridge University Press (1966)
8   Nzekwu, Onuora. Eze Goes to School. African Universities Press (1966)

Do not get me wrong; I believe that anything worth doing is worth doing well. I believe in doing what it takes to get the job done. So even if I had become a mechanic, I would be the best damn mechanic in town. It is all about attitude and what you put into it. It is the classic statement "garbage in, garbage out" or GIGO, that is in effect and working in all our lives.

I am a firm believer that the universe gives you as much as you are willing to receive. But you show your willingness to receive by what you put in. It is not a one-way street with you just receiving; you have to be giving and doing in order to receive. Show me a man diligent in his business, and I will show you a man ready to move from grass to grace, from eating sandwiches in a paper bag alone sitting on a step, to eating a fine meal at a lakeside restaurant with his good friends. Not everyone who goes to the university receives a degree. Only people who commit to studying to prove themselves in a field of study receive a degree in that area.

Mother reckoned that whatever inconvenience one had to endure during one's sojourn as an undergraduate should be borne gallantly, as such inconvenience would be greatly compensated when one graduates with honors. And from that point forward, that hard work would be rewarded with my being gainfully employed, and, ultimately, enjoying the good things that life brings to the hard working, the diligent, and the honest. She was convinced that an excellent university grade was a harbinger of the good life, and this was the gospel she preached to all her children and anyone else who cared to listen. I believed her because she meant well and spoke out of love for her children and the life she wanted for them.

Trust me, I know what it means to be in need, and now I know what it is to have plenty; I have seen both sides. I bought into my mum's message, and I believed her when she said we would become more than we were; I ran with it. It made me face life like someone who not only knows where he was coming from but also knows where he is going. I was determined to let the wonderful end that was possible—the wonderful end that my mother believed we could achieve—determine the godly means. I say "godly means" because only wealth bestowed by God guarantees your peace. I had a mental picture of where I wanted to be in five years' time, ten years' time, and twenty years' time, and I got in that mental car and kept driving to that destination my mother had put in front of me.

But on the path, I did suffer, just like most students in Nigerian tertiary institutions, where electricity outages were, and still are, the norm. I literally burnt candles in order to study, attended lectures in overcrowded lecture theatres, copied my notes over and over as I did my assignments, and bought lecturers' handouts and textbooks at exorbitant prices. In fact, I did everything a determined student should do, and what I have to show for it today is a very hard-earned B. Eng. (First Class), MS and PhD degrees, all in Petroleum Engineering, and today a pair of recommended glasses that makes things appear brighter and clearer. Working hard, doing whatever it took to obtain my education—as my mother wanted for me—that was plan A. There was no plan B, except that plan B was to make plan A work. No matter what kind of hardship I had to endure or conquer to obtain the result, to get to my goal of becoming a global petroleum engineer of choice, someone who could work for an oil and gas company in any part of the world, that is who I had become.

Chapter 02

Becoming a Businessman

In 1990 we moved from our single room abode to two rooms along Aba/Owerri Road in Abayi, Aba, Nigeria. The size of each room was about 12-ft by 12-ft. We utilized one room as the living area and the other as the bedroom. There was a connecting door between both rooms so we could easily access one room from the other. It was a welcomed upgrade in living standards for us but similar to the compound where we had our single room abode, the living facilities (kitchen, restrooms, bathrooms, etc.) were shared with other residents of the compound. It was not that easy for us to get a place because most landlords did not want to have a nuclear family of seven (my mum with her six kids) move into two rooms. They felt we were too many and could easily put a strain on the shared living facilities.

At that time, we continued to live very frugally, as we were dependent on my mum's monthly salary that was neither sufficient nor steady. I say it was not sufficient because being a civil servant as a primary school teacher did not pay enough to cover our rent and the school fees for myself and my five siblings.

Mother was strong and determined though; she sacrificed all that was necessary for us. She was focused on making sure we all got university degrees. As a matter of fact, her salary, as inconsistent as the government was in paying monthly, was spent or earmarked for someone's school fees before it was received.

None of us had graduated from college yet, so we were not in a position to help my mother with raising money in any major way to pay for things. Everyone was at one stage of education or the other. As you will see, though, we did whatever we could.

We all contributed the best we could by doing simple jobs. Farming was another great way of raising money for us; we would frequently travel to the village and harvest cassava, sell some to raise money, and make garri (a staple food in Nigeria) and sell part of the garri to raise money to pay for other things like rent, our books, and school fees. As long as we had our transportation money to go to the village, that was enough because we knew that selling cassava from the farm would generate money for our return trip. I never really looked forward to those trips to the village because I always considered them too exhausting and laborious for my liking, but remember, I was still very young and these were very long days for me. But we had to make the trip every now and then because it was how we raised money for school, and it was how we made sure we had food on the table when Mother's salary had not been paid in months, which often happened.

A few years later, a breakthrough came for us. It so happened that our neighbors were involved in a retail business that involved selling boiled eggs or bread to travelers at a nearby motor park. We watched them buy fresh crates of eggs, boil them, and take them to the motor park each day to sell. Each person ended up selling close to four crates a day. Each crate contained about 30 eggs. I could not stop asking myself, *"Don't these park people get fed up eating eggs every single day? Who are these people? They must really like eggs, and they must have a lot of money too,"* I said while chatting with Chinomso and Ugochi, my siblings. The profits were small, but it added up to good money, especially for a 12-year-old boy like me. I could do a lot with that much money. So my family asked about the business and how it worked and made a decision to get involved whenever we found the time.

However, mother would not let us stay away from school in order to make money. School activities always came first, even if it meant doing so on an empty stomach because there was nothing in the house to eat. But during weekends and holidays when people travel, the motor parks were usually packed, so those days made for good sales, and we took advantage of those days to make money. At first, I did this with two of my siblings to supplement Mother's income, and later on it was a great source of income for me to generate money to fund my education. It was not easy at first. I felt kind of weird begging people to buy stuff. I was used to being the one purchasing bread from hawkers when we were travelling to the village. Now being one of them did not sit so well with me, so the first few times I sold things did not go so well. But being someone who always strives to be the best in whatever I do, I got the hang of it, and before long, I was making good sales, positioning myself well and always finishing the sale of my produce in good time.

Because I was neat and presented my produce in the best possible way that I could, it helped me stand out from other hawkers, and being educated, I could easily communicate with anyone. I looked different; I carried myself differently. I had focus. Yes, I was one of the boiled-egg hawkers, but I knew I was not there to make that my trade. It was a means to an end. I saw being successful at selling eggs as the only way for me to move ahead into the life I wanted and that my mother wanted for my siblings and me.

I recall some days while raising money to buy the books I needed for school that were painful for me. Even as a senior in high school, some junior students that saw me called me names. Some called me

Doing Better Than Your Best

"Nwa-akwa" (meaning egg seller or egg boy), which is a name that customers normally call people that sell boiled eggs at the motor park. It was fine to be called "Nwa-akwa" when someone was calling you to buy eggs, and it even makes you happy. I would get excited that I was about to sell my produce. In fact, if I did not respond in a timely manner, there were five or more "Nwa-akwa" traders, just like me, who would come running towards "my" customer to convince him to buy their eggs instead of my eggs.

Some of the egg sellers would bring out their biggest eggs to lure the customers to them, and some would say that their eggs were still hot. There were all kinds of patter thrown at the person that called out the name Nwa-akwa. So you had better be quick and have the biggest eggs or have a customer that was focused on buying from you or they would buy from the other person selling eggs. Soon I learned to respond to the name gladly and with joy and happiness when selling in the motor park. The egg sales meant a better future for me.

But that same name became derogatory and offensive when I was dressed for school and someone who knew I retailed eggs during the weekends or during the holidays began to call me Nwa-akwa. Calling to me with this name then meant it was mockery and meant to be painful and hurt my feelings. So when I was dressed up and looking good and strolling on the road and I was feeling good about myself, to hear a voice come out from the buildings or when I was walking by children playing on the streets that would call out to me, "Nwa-akwa," I was hurt. But I also knew that they just wanted to make fun of me. I knew if they could make me more concerned about what they thought of me than I was about my future, then I would lose my focus on my goal. This, too, would be a way of "associating" with those that cannot inspire you to be successful and the kind of people my mother warned us about.

As you can see, those were difficult times for me, but I did not let them stop me. I sold boiled eggs at the motor park whenever the need was there for me to raise money for the family's greater good. I did not see selling eggs as an end or something that I would be doing in five or ten years' time. Rather, I was using this as an opportunity to work towards the future that I had always dreamt about and that my mother so wanted for her children. I was working towards a future, and selling eggs was just a godly means to an end. Hawking was Plan B to help make Plan A work. But do not think this did not hurt at the time. It felt very shameful to me even though I knew why I was doing it. I did not take it personally or let it control my choices, because I knew I was not going to be an egg seller forever. I knew it was just for the "now" and was a temporary situation that I would move past. It was my means to my end.

I felt that they could say whatever they liked, call me names that hurt, but I did not care. I kept telling myself that I would not always be there with them. Very soon, I would be driving my own luxurious car, and they would be rushing to sell their goods to me. I hoped that they would be able to recognize me then and know that my means had brought me my successful end.

Even as the best student in my class in college, I still looked out for opportunities to raise money during the holidays, be it teaching at private elementary schools or selling bread during Christmas or any holiday. These were all decisions that I made in the past, which looking back on, I cannot help but thank God for his great provisions and guidance for us and for my mom. Like all small children, on occasion, I would complain to Mum that I could not do this any longer, as it was not easy to do, but mother always encouraged me. She never failed to let me know that if I did not feel like going that day that I could take the day off to take a moment out and gather my strength. Eventually, I stopped hating poverty, knowing that it was just a temporary position. Things were going to turn around for me and be better if only I could stay the course, do the dos, and let situations and circumstances unfold from the work I was putting in.

On a trip back to Aba, Nigeria, during the summer of 2013 after eight years of being away, our car drove past the motor park area where I used to hawk boiled eggs and bread. I saw new faces there

Doing Better Than Your Best

selling eggs and bread, and I also saw old faces, people that I once fought with over getting the customers. They are still there, selling eggs and bread from different bakeries, and some now have small stores on the roadside. Call them an upgrade, an expansion even, these small roadside stores. But just as I predicted, here I am 10 years later, and I am driving on the road, and when I pull over, they are rushing to our car to sell their produce to me. Oh, and if you are wondering if I talked to the young ones among them, yes, I did. "Make sure you take school seriously. Let this, selling eggs, be your means to an end. Please don't see it as the end point. I was once like you but I never gave up on school. Today I hold a doctorate degree in engineering. When you get home, you may be tired, but pick up your books and read. Study to be the best in your class," I urged them.

I offered this advice to them just as my mother had offered it to me—and as I now offer it to you.

Let the End Determine the Means

Your conduct reflects your self-image. Arnold Schwarzenegger[9] could not even speak English when he moved to the USA. When asked how he became the governor of the State of California, he rightfully said that he had a picture of where he wanted to be and lived his life to get there. He practically made his way to the top. In an interview published in *Hemisphere* magazine, a Houston-based first flight officer, Donald Turner[10] reiterated that becoming a pilot was what he wanted to do. There was no plan B, except that plan B was to make plan A work. Donald Turner says *"I hear statistics that only six percent of the population is doing what they really love. I fit in with the six percent, but I can relate to the 94%. Sometimes you have to do a lot of what you don't want to do to get to do what you want to do."* This

---

9 Arnold Schwarzenegger is an Austrian American actor, politician, businessman, investor, and former professional bodybuilder.
10 Averyly Re. Pursuing Plan A. Hemisphere Magazine (September 2011) http://www.hemispheresmagazine.com/2011/09/01/pursuing-plan-a/

perspective is powerful, and when you understand it, you will go places. Understand that you need to let the end determine the means. *"Things like that humble you because they let you know that you are always being watched. I always try to put my best foot forward,"* he continued. I love that; it kind of puts everything in perspective for me. There was no plan B except that every other plan was to make plan A succeed. That is a doing better than your best mentality.

To me, plan A was to graduate with excellent grades from college, get a good job in the oil and gas industry, and live the good life. I found out what was required to achieve this and did something each day that drove me towards achieving my goal. Be it paying attention to my studies, studying for my exams, making sure I raised money to pay my school fees, completing all my assignments in school, you name it, I did it with joy. That is the mind-set that is required. Even powerful faith cannot accomplish your dreams until you take action. Your dreams must be hooked up with actions or they will go nowhere. You can have a dream, believe God's word, even soak it in prayer and plan or lay it out, but until you begin to move toward that dream, you will never see any results. As the Bible states, *faith without works is dead*[11].

Some people have dreams but do not believe these dreams will become realities. Other people have dreams and believe they will come to pass, but they never pray concerning their dreams. Then some have dreams, believe, pray, and plan, but they never act upon their dreams. The attainment of your dreams is not only based on belief and prayer but on the amount of active faith you release—not passive faith but active faith. I have faith to agree with you that every dream you have is going to come to pass even as you begin to set your dream into motion. Let the end justify the means, but always follow the words of Martin Luther King Jr., "Means we use must be as pure as the ends we seek."[12]

---

11 See James 2:26
12 King Jr, Martin Luther, "Letter from a Birmingham Jail" 16 April 1963 http://www.africa.upenn.edu/Articles_Gen/Letter_Birmingham.html

Chapter **03**

My Academic Pursuit of Excellence

"I didn't fail. I only discovered several ways by which it was impossible to generate an incandescent lamp." - Thomas Edison[13]

One thing that I have learned about life is that people who persevere to succeed in life pay as much attention to their mistakes as they do to their accomplishments. They learn from their failed attempts and either try harder the next time or readjust their energy toward a more passionate goal. I call it Thomas Edison's mentality. Until you see the reason behind your failure, you will continue to fail, i.e., you will not attain success. For instance, if you can figure out the reason why it happened—if you can figure out the reason why you did not get an "A" in freshman general studies (GST) 101 course and work

---

13 Thomas Edison (February 11, 1847 – October 18, 1931) was an American inventor and businessman. The popular quote comes from an interview with Edison that was published in the January 1921 issue of the American Magazine.

on closing that gap, you will be able to make "A" in GST 102. If you discover the reason why you did not meet your grade expectations in freshman mathematics (MTH) 101 and work on it, you will be able to excel in MTH 102.

No one is better than you; no one is smarter than you. If someone is doing better than you are today, it simply means that they are doing a better job of learning not just from their mistakes but also from other people's failures. According to Brian Tracy, people have learnt how cause and effect affects their work, and they have applied it.[14] If you do not like the way something has been going on in your life, think your way out of it; do not just tolerate it. I recall when I always forgot my company badge at home whenever I was in a rush to leave home. I had to frequently visit the safety and security department/desk to get a temporary identity card that allowed me to gain access to my office building. I had to think myself out of it. I made a wise decision to always put my identity card inside my laptop bag whenever I got home from work. That way, when I pick up my laptop bag in the morning because I cannot go to work without it, I know I also have my badge with me. With this approach, I have not visited the security desk for more than three years. This used to occur about once a week.

The achievement of personal excellence is a decision that you make or fail to make. No one becomes excellent accidentally; failing to commit to a life of excellence in your chosen career will automatically default you to average performance, if not mediocrity. One of my notable life skills is an unwavering pursuit of excellence. I have it written on my resume. My true confession is that success requires planned hard work. Great success is found through diligent efforts. Diligence involves investing your abilities, strength, and all you have into the pursuit of your mission. Lazy and idle people never make any headway in life because they are not using one of God's formulas for successful living: *diligence.*[15]

---

14 Tracy, Brian. No Excuses!: The Power of Self-Discipline, Vanguard Press (May 25, 2010)
15 Proverbs 22:29

In my experience in the oil and gas industry, a great deal of work is done and several committees are routinely set up to investigate why certain projects are not completed as scheduled. Here is a brief description of an oil and gas industry problem solving situation that affirms the significance of this kind of reasoning. The issue occurred while drilling an oil well. With the surface casing (metallic pipes used to secure wellbores before drilling further) in place, the team drilled down to the intermediate casing set point and pulled out of the hole in order to run the next casing string. Several attempts were made to lay this metallic pipe through this open-hole section without success, a process usually referred to as casing and used to isolate the drilled intervals before drilling further to reach the hydrocarbon bearing formations. This intermediate section was made up of a 9.5 inches diameter casing to be run through an open hole created by a 12.5 inches diameter drilling bits. This is a routine operation carried out by the rig crew. It should go easily without any hitches. However, if there were problems, such as walls of the hole collapsing and reducing the diameter of the open hole if not closing it up entirely, then it could be a long day with a significant amount of troubleshooting and non-productive time. An operation planned to be completed within 72 hours could then take more than two weeks due to the accumulated non-productive times. After several failed attempts, the team decided to drill through whatever was causing the blockage. They tried this over and over again until they all came to the conclusion that the prior established open hole had been lost. This could be due to swelling shale that had been exposed to the drilling fluids, or it could be due to some other form of wellbore instability, such as hole collapse, wall cave-ins, and what have you. The well was then placed on temporary abandonment, and a high-powered committee was established and tasked with the job of discovering why the well could not be completed. In the months that followed, several highly skilled engineers and scientists were flown in from around the globe to partake in a brainstorming session to analyze all that could have contributed to the events in this well. Several third party companies were also consulted to analyze available data and present their views on the probable cause of the problem.

As an intern, I was privileged to sit in a few of the brainstorming sessions. The process involved going through the timeline of events that occurred, evaluating the technology employed to drill this well, and also attempting to answer obvious questions such as what were the recommended procedures followed and how do the actual drilling fluids measure up with the pre-job design? Answers were sought to all these questions and more to arrive at a new proposal to achieve the set goal. As a result of the root cause failure analysis conducted, subsequent wells were successfully drilled and completed, confirming the words of Napoleon Hill, who stated and I quote, "When defeat comes, accept it as a signal that your plans are not sound, rebuild those plans, and set sail once more toward your coveted goal."[16]

While it is not my intention to turn this into an engineering exercise, I would like to drive home the fact that one can learn a lot when things do not go the way you expected. The answer is right there with you. You just have to dig in to find it. Sometimes you have to dig really deep; some other times you know the answer even before you start digging. I have said it before, and I will say it again: success requires planned hard work. Hard work will take you to the top. A hard worker presses on in spite of all odds.

Throughout my life, I have always chosen to invest my abilities, strength, and all I have into the pursuit of my mission. It goes with my unwavering pursuit of excellence. It holds true to the saying that lazy and idle people never make any headway in life because they are not using God's formula for successful living. Everyone who will receive the prize requires an inner drive for an outward mark. It is time to challenge yourself to achieve.

---

16   Hill, Napoleon. Think and Grow Rich. Tarcher; Rev Exp Edition (August 18, 2005)

My Academic Life

There is a feeling that comes with being the best student in your class, a feeling I grew accustomed to from my childhood days—having been at the top of my class for the most part of my academic life. I had my worst grade in primary one, placing outside the top ten students. My mum was not happy with me, because she required us to be top in our class. That was the commitment she desired from her children. This time she was lenient on me because it was my first stint in school and I was the youngest in my class. I was barely four years old, and I was in class with older kids who had completed two or more years of nursery education. That was probably the only time I placed outside the top five students in my class. For the most part, I always had my eye on the first position. That was Mum's goal, and it later became mine. Any other placement was considered failure, including being the second or third best student in the class, by (reluctantly) myself and more especially my confident mum.

Before my junior secondary school certificate examination (JSSCE), I was a local champion. You cannot count the best three students in my class (Junior Secondary School Class 3F – 1993) at Ngwa High School, Aba, Nigeria, without mentioning my name. On August 21, 1993, I received my JSSCE results. I had a distinct three coaches and seven players. For those of you who are still wondering what that means, a "coach" refers to having a "C" grade, while a "player" refers to having an ordinary "pass" grade in your exam. I could not compare myself to other students who were cruising their nine (9) distinctions, eight (8) distinctions, seven (7) distinctions and several other excellent results. I was disappointed with myself, so I asked myself why. Why did I not make the type of results that my colleagues were making? I went into deep thought and found out these truths:

(a) *Inadequate materials:* Because I did not have access to relevant textbooks due to my financial status, I relied mostly on my class note books. This was not helpful during the exam because I encountered several words, phrases, clauses, sentences, and even diagrams that I had never seen in any of my class note books. To make matters worse, I was being asked to either define these words or write a short note about them. Tell me, how could I? Preparing for exams, one must make sure he/she understands the exam coverage—do not be a local champion for an exam that requires national or global coverage. My experience in graduate school also helped me realize the importance of having adequate background information. Knowing the fundamentals is key. As someone with a petroleum engineering background, the graduate study course work in petroleum engineering was easier for me to grasp than it was for my colleagues who had a background in chemical, mechanical, or electrical engineering. This was also evident for me when I sat in a graduate level mathematics coursework and was using pages to solve a mathematics problem that mathematics majors in the same class were solving in just a few lines. They had the adequate background information, so they were using mathematical short-cuts and established methodologies that were above me. It pays to have the right background knowledge.

(b) *My answers were too brief:* Concerning the theoretical questions, I rejoiced over every familiar question on the examination, but in each of them, it was difficult to produce more than two sentences as my answer. So I believed that it must have affected my grades. Later, as an employee of the agency that conducts the senior secondary certificate examinations, I was assigned the task of making sure all the points awarded to a candidate were rightfully added to ensure that the correct grade was assigned to the student. Being a part of this board helped me realize how the marking system works and affirmed my notion that giving brief answers without explanations affected the number of points one could be awarded. Reviewing the grading or marking scheme confirmed that one could score points for definitions, additional points for explanations (thank God for synonyms), and some more points for correct answers and examples using practical illustrations or real life examples (depending on the subject). For instance, if one is asked to briefly describe your understanding of the meaning of success, a simple and correct answer could be that success is the attainment of a set goal. One could go a little further by stating that success means different things to different people. What is considered success by one could be a failure for another individual. Using teams in the NBA league in the United States as an example, while the Los Angeles Lakers basketball team will not consider making it to the playoffs and getting knocked out as a successful season, an upcoming team with young talents could set a goal of just making it to the play-offs as their measure of success. If you are a soccer fan, you can easily relate with fans of Manchester United requiring them to win the Barclays English Premier League each year, while the fans of a different team will rejoice greatly if their team made it into a spot that qualifies them for any European competition. Adding such real life illustrations to your response to questions helps you connect with the examiner, and you get awarded points that you could easily have missed.

(c) *Use of past questions and answers:* The place for past questions and answers to academic excellence became clear to me when I found out that two of my three credits in JSSCE were on integrated science and social studies—two subjects that I had access to past questions and answers. So I told myself, "Had it been that you had past questions and answers in all these subjects, you would have made up to ten credits." I nodded my head, my way of accepting that I just made a very important discovery that will impact my academic pursuit going forward. Be assured that I made a decision about this; a decision to seek out or sort and review solutions to all past questions that I could get for subjects and courses in my future academic pursuits.

(d) *Memorization:* The human brain needs memorization to develop. As Dr NakaMats, the inventor of floppy disk, compact disk, compact disk player, digital watch, and water powered engines rightly states: *"If you don't learn how to memorize effectively, you can't reach your full potential."*[17] If a child does not learn how to memorize effectively, he or she does not reach his or her full potential. That is how geniuses are formed. Knowing this, I chose to use every spare opportunity that came my way to memorize the definition and meaning of words. For instance, if I was going to take 30 minutes to walk to church on a Sunday morning, I would endeavor to write down the definition of new words or scientific terms on a piece of paper and would make it a habit to read and memorize these write ups on my way to and from church. I followed the same approach if I was taking a taxi on my way to school, church, market, visit friends, or anywhere for that matter. Too often we allow the pain and perspiration of reading to hide its blessings. We assume that reading is a necessary evil without looking for the good it brings. I encourage you to be futuristic in your attitude towards reading. It worked for me, and it can work for you too.

I Made a Decision

My JSSCE examination result was decent enough that I got placed in SS1 A. This was a class for the best science students. I was troubled

---

17 NakaMats, Yoshiro. Also known as Dr. NakaMats is a Japanese inventor. The quote comes from an interview that was published in Charles "Chic" Thompson's *What a Great Idea*, Harper Perennial (January 2, 1992).

because I saw myself as inferior to those people that had mostly "A"s in their JSSCE. Being competitive, I had a plan and knew what I had to do. How you view the problems and situations around you determines the use to which you will put your mind. If you see yourself as being capable of handling it, your mind will go to work and ultimately find a way out of the problem. I worked on the truths I found out concerning my JSSCE. I went for every relevant textbook I could lay my hands on. I bought practical textbooks and past questions and answers and really made use of them. You are probably wondering how I got the money for these books. Friends, how would you value a gift of the best chemistry textbook as your birthday gift, a nice physics textbook for your Christmas gift, and a scientific calculator for your holiday package? That was part of the decision I made.

Moreover, I used money that came my way for my unwavering pursuit of academic excellence. I worked during holidays and after school hours some days. It was too demanding, not in vogue, and humiliating to do at times. It brought all sorts of insults my way—remember Nwa Akwa from my story earlier—but I had the future in view. My mind was made up for a bright future, one that could be achieved through academic excellence by the grace of God. I had many options, but I chose a life with a bright future. I did not care about how dignified the means were. I set my eyes on the goal. I was so focused on letting the godly means justify and determine the end.

Most people want to be students, but they do not want to read. They want the pleasure, but they do not want to expend the energy. Nothing is as depressing and frustrating as a student that is not interested in studying or reading. This attitude is completely contrary to God's gift of knowledge. Study to prove yourself. A workman needs not to be ashamed. A lot of missed leisure time, play hours, and dates had allowed me to focus on preparing for my final exams, including my senior secondary school certificate examination (SSSCE) in 1996. I studied through the holidays; I had a study group of three students. We met in school every day during vacations and weekends (including Sunday evenings after church service). We studied until we got exhausted and could no longer continue for the day. We exhibited focus; we solved problems. We covered all grounds. Even when I got home, I would eat dinner and continue with my studies. When there was no electricity, I used lamps and candles. I did not want to have a repeat of my JSSCE result. I was not about to be a local champion again. I wanted to be ready for the exam, so I covered all possible grounds. I reviewed all past questions and made sure I could solve them all. I crammed formulas, learned short-cuts, and memorized words and definitions of high importance.

By the time the exam period came, I was ready—ready for any question that could be thrown at me and ready for the nine subjects I had registered for. I am not sure if I was ever ready for English and the test of oral English. I never really took time to study the English language as a subject. I felt if I can speak the language, I can write essays, read, and answer comprehension questions and fill in the blanks with synonyms and antonyms, that was good enough to pass the subject. Bad attitude. It was good enough, but I had my worst grade (an acceptable credit) in English. This occurred because I did not pay adequate attention to studying the English language. For other subjects, I studied to an extent that some days, while studying in the living room, my mum would come and switch off the lights in order to force me to go to bed and get some rest. Hearing her say, *"My son, it's 4:00 a.m. in the morning, and you are still studying. Please, that's enough for today; get some rest. You can continue tomorrow,"* with a mother's voice usually served as a sign for me to call it a day. It became a norm. That is one thing with me; I am such a driven person that if I am making headway in what I am doing, sleep or hunger cannot stop me. I can go for hours nonstop. I developed this self-discipline over time, which really helped me in the future when I was completing my dissertation that required going days without sleep, more often than not. It was not too difficult, because I had done it before. It was not the right thing to do either, because on occasion I would break down and lose a couple of days, days I could have used to get some rest.

When you do well in an exam, you know even before the grades are published. I knew I was prepared when our SSSCE mock results came out and my grades were among the best in my school. As a matter of fact, I had the highest score in most of the subjects. As I reviewed my mock exam results, the feeling of being ready overwhelmed me. I was ready for the real deal. I could feel it. When the time came, I entered the exam hall, and I was cool, calm, and collected so I would not make any mistakes. When you get into an examination hall, you see all kinds of students. I have been in too many examinations not to notice the disparity amongst students in the exam hall. There are different kinds of people in the exam hall. Some are there just to pass; some are there to make a comfortable grade, while some are there to make an excellent grade. Some are prepared, and some are not. There are a few very talented or skillful students, some highly motivated students that have put in extra hours of preparation, and some that just do not care or get it. Some are ready for the questions to be distributed to them, while some are trying to figure out who they will be copying their answers from. They have not seen the questions yet, but they already know they cannot answer them. Deep within many, they believe that the secret might be hard work, so they are afraid. But I like to say one thing—what is true about many things in life is true about reading: The more you do it, the easier it becomes and the easier it is for you to extract information from any printed page.

I had an interesting experience during my SSSCE biology exam. A fellow student, Emeka, told me to help him or he would beat me up at the end of the examination if I did not. Judging by his notorious behavior on campus, I could not call this an empty threat. He was known to exhibit such behavior. Being the quiet type, I never looked for trouble, and here I was in the exam hall, with someone requesting that I copy my answers on a piece of paper for him. Within me, I was fighting two incompatible emotions: the scare of getting waylaid and beat up on my way home and a conscious effort to avoid getting involved in examination malpractice. I did not know what to do; it affected my concentration and focus, and before I knew it, I began to cry. I could feel tears dropping down my cheeks, and one of my teachers, Mr. Amadi, noticed it and came to me. Mr. Amadi was respected among the students. I informed him of the development, and he seriously warned the student. I was taken out of the hall to the corridor of the class to write my exam alone. It was lonely but peaceful. When the external examiner came to me, he thought I was giving trouble inside the hall that led to invigilators taking me out of the exam hall to write the exam alone in the corridor. He was giving me a hard time until one of the teachers came and informed him that I was taken outside to prevent other students from copying my work. Thankfully, I had given my best efforts in most of the questions that I answered, and looking through my paper, I felt good for the instructor that would be grading my paper. Knowing that I had done an excellent job, I was happy. I prayed. God answered. By the time my senior secondary school certificate examination (SSSCE) results were out, I made eight distinctions and one credit (English language). This was not just the best result in my school but the best result among my peers in the whole city.

Chapter 04

Getting University Admission

God has raised men to help me along the way to achieve my goals and fulfill my destiny. I say this because though I was the best graduating student in my secondary school, Ngwa High School Aba, with eight distinctions and a credit, getting admission into the university was not a cake walk. For my first JAMB (Joint Admissions and Matriculation Board—Nigerian equivalent to SAT in the United States), I registered to take mathematics, physics, and chemistry to gain admission into the university to study Electrical and Electronics Engineering. After my SSSCE result came out, everyone saw me as a medical student; uncles, friends, neighbors, church members, and everyone who cared enough to contribute to my career decision making process. My family and I were convinced that I should become a medical doctor. My high school results were too good for me not to pursue a career in the medical profession. Medical doctors are well respected in Nigerian society because they make good money. I did not have anything against becoming a doctor.

Moreover, while preparing for SSSCE with my study colleagues at my high school one weekend, we met a third year medical student who came to the same location to study while he was on vacation, and he spoke of me as someone who would make an excellent medical student. He stated this because I was able to answer his questions on most parts of the body, including the human skeletal system. So when the push came for me to switch from engineering to medical school, I easily agreed and went ahead to replace mathematics with biology for my JAMB examination. I took the exam and scored 216. The highest score that year was 261. I put in for Medicine and Surgery at University of Nigeria Nsukka (UNN), and the cut off mark for admission was 241. I did not gain admission that year. I did not even bother visiting the college of medicine at the University of Nigeria Nsukka (UNN), the school to which I had submitted the admission application. I was later informed that if I had visited, the head of the department could have offered me admission based on my SSSCE result. I did not know that; I just gave up, and no one advised me about what to do.

The next year, I went back to my engineering. This time I registered for petroleum engineering (PE) with Federal University of Technology Owerri (FUTO) as my first choice and University of Benin (UNIBEN) as my second choice. I took the JAMB exam and had an improved score of 266/400. The highest score that year was more than 300. I waited a couple of months for the cut-off mark to be admitted into my chosen schools. This time, I made visiting FUTO a routine. I even met with the head of the petroleum engineering department, Dr. Obah, and showed him my SSSCE result along with my JAMB score. He was impressed with my academic achievements. He informed me that I was likely going to be below the cut-off mark for the department, but nevertheless, he would like to admit me. He was not impressed by the students he had been meeting, students who had excellent JAMB results with no corresponding SSSCE result.

There were many students who had to combine two or more SSSCE results to meet the requirements for admission, but they had scored above the required cut-off mark for admission into the program, far above my score. It was clear that most of them possibly cheated in their JAMB examination. He feared that they would not necessarily do well in the program. This event confirmed my thoughts about not visiting the college of medicine at UNN. I felt bad that I never visited to speak with the head of the department after I missed the cut-off mark in the previous year. It was wrong. One should never give up on their dreams. Give it your best shot, and hang in there until you have done all you can do. Giving up should not have been an option. I might have given up because it was not really my dream. I was practically chasing a dream that everyone had chosen for me.

Back to my head of department (HOD), Dr. Obah informed me to visit the Vice Chancellor (VC) of the institution through any means I could and see if he would offer me admission into the petroleum engineering program. The VC is the highest ranking administrative and educational head in Nigerian universities. Dr. Obah stated that the VC was my only hope of getting into the program as things stood. Just as he stated, the admission list came out, and I was not shortlisted. The general cut-off for petroleum engineering was 275, and the cut off for people from my State (Abia) was 268. I missed admission by two points.

When I saw the list without my name on it, I was depressed. I did not know what to do; I was almost in tears. I could not call home because we did not have cell phones then. My family had to wait for me to return to get the news. I was not about to spend another year at home. I was not cut out for that kind of life. Studying for the same exam again! No! I cried out. I prayed to God to make a way for me. I fasted, my Mum fasted, and every member of my family prayed for my admission. Friends advised me to apply for supplementary admission into a different program. I refused. I believed that God would make a way for me. I was so sure, the same way I was sure about my SSSCE result, that I did not register for the general certificate of education (GCE – an equivalent of SSSCE) examination. I placed all my hope in realizing my dream of being admitted into the petroleum engineering department at FUTO. I knew God could do it. How he was going to do it, I did not know.

The option I had for admission was finding someone who could get the attention of the Vice Chancellor. During this challenging time, I went to visit my older brother, Chiemela, who was a student at the University of Calabar. Together, we tried to think of who we could ask to visit the VC with me and who God could use to speak to the VC about offering me admission into the PE program, a highly sought after department in FUTO. We later agreed that going to Justice Emeka, a once prominent member of our local church and a distant relative who was recently appointed and sworn in as a Federal High Court judge would be an excellent start. He knew my family, so we believed that he would be eager and willing to support my quest for admission. Eager and willing he was.

He did not volunteer to visit FUTO with me to meet with the Vice Chancellor of my alma mater, but he wrote a very powerful letter of request, right in front of me. I loved the content. He placed a seal of the Federal High Court on it. My duty was to deliver the letter to the VC's office. He also wrote another letter to Mr. Ukomadu, a high ranking officer at FUTO, who was his fellow alumni from his university days. I took both letters to Mr. Ukomadu, and he offered to deliver the VC's letter to his office. I enquired if there was something I needed to do to ensure that the VC would give the letter the attention that it deserved; he categorically told me not to bother. We had done our part, and it was left for the VC to do his. Then I knew that it was time for me to go back to my prayer room; from that day until the VC's list came out, I did not allow any day to pass without praying for a favorable consideration of the request.

The day came when the VC's list was released, and I travelled to campus to check for my name on the list. This was early December

1998. Students that got admission from the first list or got in through supplementary admission had already begun lectures in October. I had missed more than four weeks of lectures while waiting to gain admission into the program. I was waiting for the VC's list, which by God's grace was my last resort. When I got to school that day, I went straight to the chemical engineering department to check if my name was on the VC's list. As I scanned through the list, I could not find my name. I was shocked. Did it mean that God did not answer my prayers? In my mind, I began to ask God, why? How could God allow this to happen to His beloved son? I know you could be wondering, why did he go to the chemical engineering department to check for admission? Didn't he apply to study petroleum engineering?

You see, Justice Emeka made a request for me to be granted admission into the chemical engineering department instead of my earlier choice of petroleum engineering (PE). He asked me why I wanted PE, and I informed him that my dream was to work in the oil and gas industry. He advised me that PE was too narrow, only meant for the oil industry. What if oil runs out, he queried me. What if you do not get a place in the oil industry? I was so sure that there would be a place for me in the oil industry, but I just needed to gain admission at this point, so whether chemical or petroleum engineering, I did not really mind. I agreed to go for chemical engineering after he gave me examples of chemical engineers who currently worked in the oil and gas industry. He advised that it was better to study chemical engineering; that way if the oil industry fails, I would have another career path to follow. I accepted, and he went ahead to seek the indulgence of the VC to offer me admission into the chemical engineering program at FUTO. So when my name was not shortlisted for the chemical engineering department, it was obvious I had missed admission again. Or so I thought. However, I walked to the petroleum engineering department, looked at the list, and behold, my name was there! God did answer my prayers!

Chapter  05

Preparing for Exams

Do not prepare for exams, rehearse for exams. That is my attitude towards examination. If you do not know the rules of the game, it is possible to learn a lot and still receive low grades. It is also possible to learn very little and receive high grades. There is really no big secret to how you do this. All it takes is figuring out what will be on tests and what kind of answers your teachers expect. One thing I always do when I am taking a new class or course is to talk to people who have taken the class before me. I try to learn from the experience of others. I ask questions, such as what does the lecturer want, and what does he or she expect? I try as much as possible to get every bit of information that I will need to do well in the course. Do not just go to people you know and people you consider friends. There is an "anointing" about people that scored over 90% or made an "A" that just rubs off on you. They do not have to be your friends; still follow them. Learn from the best, not just the accessible.

Doing Better Than Your Best

On teamwork, I like to study with other dedicated students. That is a winning attitude. It is a top performer's attitude. Not all the time though; studying in a group is mostly after I have completed my personal studies. It pays when other members of the study group have completed their private studies too. That way, we get together to discuss our opinions and what we gleaned from our individual studies. From my experience, some people do not really do their own individual studies before coming for group studies; most times I get to be the one teaching the group what I know or sharing my solutions with the group. This helps too because I can recall situations where friends found errors in my answers and I was able to adjust so as not to make the same mistake in the exam hall. It pays to have friends who can critique your work, not just people who are there to accept whatever you offer. We could help each other understand the parts that are hard for us. As I described earlier, while preparing for my SSSCE (High School) examinations, I had regular group studies with two friends: Mark and Chimaobi. We set problems and questions, solved them, and compared our solutions and answers. Occasionally, I learnt new techniques of solving problems from them. At times they also learnt from me. We discussed differences in our solutions to reach an agreement on what works best.

I loved studying; the more I enjoyed reading, the more I went to study with my friends. The more capacity I developed to study, the more fun it was to study. Please hear me say it again; deep down many people believe that the secret might be hard work, so they allow themselves to get scared. The truth remains that what is true about many things in life is true about reading; the more you do it, the easier it becomes and the easier it is for you to extract information from any printed page. Studying, to me, was more fun than stress because of the knowledge that I gained from it. I got better each day and better prepared for my forthcoming exams. I tried not to put off till tomorrow what I could accomplish today. My thought was that by the time I got to tomorrow, there would be other things to do and new things to learn. Procrastination robs you of your joy. It makes for a stressful lifestyle, bringing the ups and downs of life. Getting better meant learning something new each day. I made sure to do that. I had textbooks that I was reading; I kept asking myself questions and answering them. Those were days I look back to and I want to relive the same again and again. This approach worked for me not only in high school but also in university and graduate school.

When I took Fluid Flow in Porous Media during my PhD program at the University of Oklahoma, my group study helped a great deal. We solved a lot of the questions that were in the recommended text book. We were basically rehearsing for the midterm exam. We solved as many problems as we could locate in the textbook; the big surprise came when we got into the exam hall, and lo and behold, about three of the four questions that came were among the problems that we had previously solved. Inside the examination hall, there were only few people smiling; my colleague and I were among them. Your guess is as good as mine on what grade we made in that course. I followed the same approach in all my courses during my master's degree program at the University of Alaska and my PhD degree program at The University of Oklahoma. All through my five years in graduate college, I never made any grade below an "A". So I had a perfect 4.0 GPA, not by preparing for exams but by rehearsing for exams. I do not consider myself ready for an exam until I have completely understood solutions to the problems or questions that were developed through the course of my studies.

To manage my time for private studies, I assigned a whole day to a subject. I read all day about that subject, no matter what other classes I had that day. Any opportunity to study was meant for the subject on my reading schedule. Of course, more difficult courses or subjects got allotted extra days. I refused to be one of those students who wasted time and then complained that they did not have enough time. It pays to be focused. I once heard this proverb: When you chase three rats going in three different directions, you end up catching none. The easiest way to lose your focus is to have another focus. I focused on one subject or course each day. It made all the difference, helping achieve my goal of recreating my life through academic excellence. I believed what my pastor once stated, and I quote: *"If you refuse to be distracted, your distracters will soon be attracted."* [18]

To rehearse for examinations, instead of revising my notes continually, I spent most of my time solving different types of problems or providing answers to questions in a written form. Practicing this way helped me decipher some of the underlying features and patterns of a concept or technique and helped me develop a feel for them. To get focused and get my mind in a problem solving groove, I solved the problems on paper, not just in my head. Also, I came to the realization that some problems that may appear easy to solve actually required me to study more to ensure that I was able to provide answers that I felt good about. My thought from this experience was that it was better to find out prior to entering an exam hall at my own convenience rather than finding out that a question I thought would be easy to solve had some challenges that would have required further studies. I formed a habit of ensuring an ability to proffer a comfortable answer to any probable question that could be in any of my exams on paper before the examination day. That meant I had to be willing to make sacrifices. My limited finances, my leisure time, everything was on the line. I was ready and willing to acquire all the materials needed for any course to achieve this goal. Also, gathering the past questions and answers required financial input.

Back in my FUTO days, I could spend all I had in search of school materials, to purchase books, photocopy old notes, and photocopy library materials (luckily most of the past questions could be obtained from the school library). I gathered all the materials I could get and used them effectively and efficiently. I made sure I was able to solve all the problems in the past questions prior to taking the exam on

---

[18] Pastor Steve Joab stated this at a Living Faith Church Sunday morning service in Aba (1998).

that course. If I could not solve a problem, I would meet with friends and try to solve that problem as a group and try to get an answer I believed in, a solution or an answer the lecturer would like and give me full grades for. If I was not satisfied with an answer, I would seek guidance from upper class students who had taken the class before. I found out, more often than not, the good students pass through the same issue you are having, so they can relate with the challenges and questions you have and be in a position to advise you on how to go about it. They also offered advice on the best possible way to present my answers in order to get maximum grades from each instructor. I always tried to get their notes. If I could not get them outright, I typically made photocopies.

Some instructors like details, while some are only interested in the final answer. When the exam week drew near, every student in my class and even people from other departments (for general courses) came to me for materials. They knew I must have gathered every available bit of information for each course that I was taking. It was my lifestyle; it was working for me. I was not going to stop, not when it was working so well. In my final year, the week before final exams, I received so many visitors coming to collect materials to prepare for our final examination that my landlord got scared. He did not like many people coming around to avoid the possibility of them coming back later to harass people living in his compound. I informed him that these were my classmates, I respected them, and they would do none of that; they were just coming because it was exam season. By the time the exam is over, you will not see most of them again, but right now I cannot stop them. They all believe I have something they need. And I did. I could not help wondering if these people got these materials when I got them and used them to study as much as I did, would they have graduated with First Class honors like I did? Would they have performed better than their current best? I would say yes. There is always an improvement that could be made if one makes a positive change to their study habits.

I recall a very genuine question that one of my classmates asked me one day.

"How do you get all this material?" he asked. *"Are they not expensive?"* From his tone, I could sense what he was trying to say that in spite of not having a lot of money, how was I able to have access to all the study materials? I did not blame him for asking (or thinking what he was) that question; I would have asked too. It is not every day that you meet someone who can use his last pocket money, meant for lunch, to photocopy materials for his coursework. So I looked up at him and smiled. I smiled because I did not know what else to do. This guy was from a rich home; when I say rich, I mean mega rich, as in affluent home. This guy's shoes alone cost as much as everything I had on me: my bag, my textbooks, my clothes, even my undies! Let me add a stretch—he could buy me if I was to be put on sale, but he did not know how I was getting materials for the courses that we were both taking in college. It has to do with each individual's priorities. I am sure if our priorities aligned, he would know.

Praying whenever I entered any examination hall was a regular routine for me. I prayed because I know that favor is necessary for unusual success. No one can work hard enough to get everything they deserve or want. Prayer is the difference between the best we can achieve and the best God can do through us. The greatest tragedy in life is prayers that get unanswered because they remained unsaid. After you have prayed, get in the habit of reading carefully and paying attention to the details. Most careless errors are caused by misreading the problem rather than computational mistakes.

I recall how I wasted more than 30 minutes on a problem because I did not read the question carefully enough to understand what was being asked of me. This happened in my freshman year in college. By the time I realized I was going the wrong route and changed my tactics, I had already lost valuable time; instead of completely solving the required five questions out of six questions in my MTH101 examination, I only got to solve four problems. I was not happy with myself; it pained me, and it still pains me as I am typing these words and remembering what happened that day. It pains because I could solve the six questions that were in the exam paper. I guess it also hurt because my final grade was completely based on that exam, and that semester, my first semester in college, I made "A"s in all my courses except this course that I ended up with a "B" grade. I learned from that experience.

Subsequently, I made sure I understood every question before I started solving them. Going forward, I allotted equal time to problems that have equal points. Any extra time gained from one could be used on the other. I was never the one to be in a hurry to leave the exam hall. I tried as much as possible to review my solutions for any computational errors or grammatical blunders before I submitted my answer booklet. People get nervous during test conditions; I realized that this usually happened to me when I was not adequately prepared for a test. Exam hall is not the best place to start worrying about final grades. Worry is a route that leads from somewhere to nowhere. I once read this illustration about worrying: "It's like sitting on a rocking chair; it keeps you busy and occupied, but you remain in the same location." I try to just focus on the task at hand, providing answers and solutions to the questions I have been asked.

On my way to write my TOEFL exam in Lagos, Nigeria, my brother, Chiemela, who had lived in Lagos for a while and knew his way around, offered to escort me to the exam venue. We needed to be at the exam location no later than 8.30 a.m. for a 9.00 a.m. appointment. We left the house early. I could hear the bells go off from the mosque on our street for their regular morning prayers. We thought we left early, but what we did not take into consideration was the amount of traffic on the road. At first it looked as if we were not even going to make it to the exam location by 10.00 a.m.. I would have missed my exam appointment and had to forfeit the exam and fees paid for it. I would have to register again. My brother was nervous, but he never showed it. It was later, after I got back from the exam, that he confessed to me. He said he was worried that we may not make it to the exam and asked how come I was not. I told him that I prayed about it; I had already asked God to make a way for me. And that was exactly what happened; before we knew it, God made a way. The road was clear, and I got to the exam location on time. That is something about me; when I am in the right standing with God, after I make a request to Him, I stay calm no matter what the enemy throws at me. I take it that if God wants me to be there, He will make a way. If it happens, it is God; if it does not, it is also God. That is my level of faith, and He has yet to fail me.

Chapter  06

The Smart Student's Credo

At the beginning of 2005, as a petroleum engineering graduate student at the University of Alaska, I walked into the school bookstore to purchase one of the required textbooks for my engineering coursework. One book on the stacks caught my attention; the title alone drew me close to it. It was titled *What Smart Students Know*.[19] Maximum grades. Optimum learning. Minimum time. I have always seen myself as a smart student, so I was drawn to the book, my intent being to find out if this guy knew what he was talking about. For the next hour, I was flipping through this book and digesting its content. To my greatest surprise, it was as if the author was describing my study habits, putting them in words in a way that I could not have imagined. I had to buy the book. The smart student's credo is a set of beliefs or principles about school and the learning process introduced

---

19 Robinson, Adam. *What Smart Students Know*. Crown Publishers, Inc. (July, 1993)

by Adam Robinson in his book *What Smart Students Know*. Most times, I do not even put in as much time as fellow students do; I just study smarter. I then realized that I had failed in many ways to explain my experience to people; my usual answer has always been it is all God. While that is the gospel truth, this book made me realize that I owe people more.

This book is part of my awakening to that call. God has blessed me mightily in several ways, and I am so happy to be sharing this experience with you. Join me in this ride for life, and God will continually guide you through the winning lane of life. What you are about to read will enable you learn more efficiently but may require some immediate changes in your study habits, i.e., instead of reading a textbook over and over again, you will be reading it once thoroughly. Instead of taking notes on everything, you will be selecting only important information. And instead of rereading your notes all term long, you will be constantly changing and revising them; trying to reduce them eventually to a single sheet—your cheat sheet. Really, the problem is not you; it is your approach! The challenge is finding a learning method that puts you in control of the process, keeps you interested and engaged in the material you are studying, and produces a genuine understanding. See yourself as a smart student; your self-image has a powerful influence on your academic performance. For a smart student, attitude is all that matters.

The American Century Dictionary defines attitude as "opinion or way of thinking or behavior reflecting your opinion or way of thinking". May I humbly add that your attitude determines the meaning or significance you attach to events and your response to them. Your attitude determines how you experience school, what goals you set, and the techniques and strategies you choose to reach them. As a result, your attitude determines how far you reach and how well you do. Let's get something straight here; the smart student's attitude is not just having a "positive mental attitude." Rather, it is believing that you can teach yourself far better than any school possibly can and having an extraordinary attitude to approach every aspect of your schoolwork differently. Becoming a smart student means that you will have to demand more of yourself; it means you have to do more than the teacher asks you to do; and it means no more excuses.

Before we get into discussing a smart student's study habits, I would like to reiterate the importance of changing the way you see yourself. Changing your study habits is much easier than changing your attitude. Yet changing your attitude is critical to becoming a smart student. Being a smart student means taking charge and teaching yourself. It is high time we stopped depending on our teachers and take charge. The message here is no more excuses!

Learning a Smart Way

Socratic Method: The process of using questions as a means of discovering knowledge and building understanding. In this scheme, knowing what questions to ask is much more important than merely knowing answers. Once you know the questions to ask, the answers will rarely be difficult to find. Moreover, in the words of Jonas Salk, *"The answer to every problem 'pre-exists.' We need to ask the right questions to reveal the answer."*[20]

This questioning process can be taken as "dialoguing" because you are setting up an internal dialogue between yourself and the (author of the) material you are studying. By asking and answering your own questions instead of relying on someone else's, you become your own teacher. Once dialoguing becomes a habit, you will be able teach yourself any subject. That is how to take charge and take control. The key is knowing what questions to ask and when to ask them. So when you study, you are reading to answer your questions and to see if your guesses were correct. If they are not, it is a tip off that you need to re-evaluate your thinking on the subject of interest. It is

---

20 A world of Ideas with Bill Moyers, "The Science of Hope with Jonas Salk," PBS Video, 1990.

better to find out your thinking or reasoning is wrong while trying to answer a question outside the exam hall while you are rehearsing for your exams than to find out after you have taken or while you are taking the exam.

Consciously or unconsciously, all smart students ask the same basic questions when they are learning a subject. What is my purpose for reading this? What do I already know about this topic? What is the big picture? What is the author going to say next? What are the "expect questions"? What questions does this information raise for me? What information is important here? How can I paraphrase and summarize this information? How can I organize this information? How can I picture this information? What is my hook for remembering this information? How does this information fit in with what I already know? I could not agree more with Adam Robinson on the importance of repeatedly asking these basic questions while you study. These questions form the basis of learning in a smart way. It keeps you engaged and motivated. He went further to reasonably state that if you ever have a problem concentrating while studying, it is because you are not doing any active thinking that engages your mind with the material. As the wise saying goes, if you do not know where you are going and if you do not have a picture of where you are going to, everywhere you get to looks like where you want to be. Smart students' learning is self-guided. They ask their own questions. Do not just read a passage; engage in it by constantly asking questions and searching for answers.

Let's evaluate the significance of each question:

1. *What is my purpose for reading this material?* If you do not know where you are going to, everywhere you get to looks like your destination. This could be likened to finding a spouse, meeting your life partner. If you do not know what you are looking for, every person you meet is the one.

2. *What do I already know about this topic?* You could be missing some of the building blocks. To understand the new material,

most times it pays off going back to get the building blocks in place before going for the kill. It is okay to take a step back in order to take two steps forward.

3. *What is the big picture?* Here you are required to skim through the material to have a feel of the outline. Discover and understand what is most important.

4. *What is the author going to say next?* As you read, go ahead of the author and anticipate what he/she is going to say next. The point is to keep you actively involved in the material and give you feedback. Remember, as a smart student, you are reading to answer your questions and see if your guesses were correct. If they were not, it is a tip off that you need to re-evaluate your reasoning. Better done now than in the heat of the exam hall.

5. *What are the "expect questions"?* Each subject asks a unique set of questions that you need to keep in mind as you read. The sooner you determine what they are, the better. Keep them in mind as you read, and they will allow you pick out the information that is most important to understanding a specific subject.

6. *What questions does this information raise for me?* Get curious; make it your own. What does this remind me of? How? Why?

7. *What information is important here?* This depends on your purpose and what material is being used for your studies.

8. *How can I paraphrase and summarize this information?* This is where you ought to translate the author's words into your own, using as few words as you can. After you have finished taking notes on the passage, you should not need to refer to the passage any more.

9. *How can I organize this information?* See if you can create any new groups or links that make sense. This is where acronyms come in handy. I recall my experience as a member of the two consecutive University of Oklahoma PetroBowl championship teams, where we always sought to form easy to remember acronyms

to represent any pertinent list that we came across during our study and rehearsals. For instance, we had LIIINKASUVQ (Libya, Iran, Iraq, Indonesia, Nigeria, Kuwait, Algeria, Saudi Arabia, UAE, Venezuela, Qatar) to help us remember the eleven members of OPEC and VISIK (Venezuela, Iran, Saudi Arabia, Iraq, Kuwait) to recall the founding fathers of OPEC. Personally, I used this method throughout my school days, in high school, university, and graduate college. A few examples are listed below: MR NIGER + D = the eight characteristics of living things (Movement, Respiration, Nutrition, Irritability, Growth, Excretion, Reproduction, Death); ROYGBIV = the seven colors of the rainbow (Red, Orange, Yellow, Green, Blue, Indigo, Violet).

10. *How can I picture this information?* The goal here is to translate as much of the information as possible into things you can visualize. This could be symbols or pictures where possible. You might be asking, why is this important? Let's do this simple exercise; when you hear an airplane, what comes to your mind? What do you think of? My guess: a mental picture of a plane flying in the sky, not the letters a-i-r-p-l-a-n-e. Creating a real or mental picture of the contents of the material that you are studying aids your ability to retain and recall important information.

11. *What's my hook for remembering this information?* This could just as well relate to question ten. Brainstorm on what could help you remember what you need to know for test, e.g., acronyms, links, differences and similarities, etc.

12. *How does this information fit in with what I already know?* You are the best judge here.

Depending on your purpose, some questions are more important than others. Some questions overlap, and you can combine them during your studies. Some you ask simultaneously, and some you ask over and over again.

Chapter  07

Shaping Young Minds

"Train up a child in the way he should go; even when he is old he will not depart from it."[21]

During NYSC, I volunteered as a member of the HIV prevention and sex education program and became part of a group of youth service corps members dedicated to the cause. During one of my team's visits to a secondary school in Bayelsa State, Nigeria, we talked to the students about the import of abstinence to prevent HIV and other STDs as well as unwanted pregnancies. At the end of our presentation, one of the male students raised his hand to ask a question. Amazed and bewildered, we all exchanged glances amongst us, wondering what his question could be. This bold student asked us if we recommended the use of condoms to prevent HIV or

---

21 Proverbs 22:6

unwanted pregnancies. Basically, he wanted to know why we did not recommend the use of condoms, which can also serve the same purpose as abstinence.

The moderator for the program called upon me to come and provide an answer to the boy's question. "Ah…"—that was the sound that I heard within me. I opened my mouth and closed it without uttering a word, not because I did not know what to say but because I was still thinking about how to frame my answer, where to begin and how to end. I am the type of person who thinks before he speaks. That day I recall giving the assembly a short lecture about the importance of abstinence. I used my personal experience to tell a story of how best one could stay away from contracting STDs or getting a fellow student pregnant while still in school. I emphasized that those who engage in premarital sex run a high risk of contracting one of the many venereal diseases rampant today as well as the possibility of losing their fertility. I told them they were at risk of not just AIDS but other common sexually transmitted diseases, such as herpes, that have no cure. I told stories of people who have had to drop out of school because they got pregnant. I explained to them that though condoms can be used to prevent most STDs and pregnancy, there is no guarantee. It does not offer 100% protection. This is because the condom can break, and if it does, it is as bad as not using one in the first place.

Secondly, I told them that using a condom does not protect you from the emotional state of mind that being sexually active can put you through. Sex is a powerful force that can cause havoc if one is not emotionally prepared to deal with it. Like nuclear power, when used correctly, it can create boundless energy. Sex is a gift from God to give us the greatest pleasure, to help in creating a deep and rich companionship with one's partner, and for procreation of the next generation. Intimate sexual activity for young people arrests their psychological, social, and academic development and performance. This is because more often than not, adolescents are too immature to deal with their explosive sex drive, and it tends to dominate their life. I told a story of two girls in my college who always did well in school. One of them fell in love and started dating this so called romantic guy in school. This guy showered her with his loving attention, bought her gifts, and was basically spoiling her with attention. They had sex, or made love as they chose to call it, whenever they had the opportunity. She believed life was sweet.

This sweet lifestyle affected her emotional state while she was in her sophomore year in college. Someone who had excellent grades as a freshman began to struggle to pass her courses. Her friends could tell she was now living in a dream world because when they got together to study, she would be lost in thought, probably thinking about her boyfriend and their time together. She lost focus, and it affected her studies. The easiest way for someone to lose focus is when they have something else to focus on. She had a different focus. Meanwhile, her friend maintained her focus and continued to study without the emotional baggage of premarital sex. When the results came out that year, you can guess who came out at the top. She lost her position at the top.

I reiterated that the best and only method that guarantees 100% against AIDS and other sexually transmitted diseases is to preferably wait for marriage to have sex and maintain fidelity in your marriage. That is what I preached, and that is what I practiced all through college and my NYSC program. I look back today, and I do see several opportunities where I could have fallen, but God guided me. He saw me through, and He always made a way for me. He always raised men as angels and angels as men to help me realize my dreams and goals in life. That is what happens when you serve Him and allow Him to be in charge of who you become, what you do, the decisions you make, where you go, who you marry, who you date, etc. This is my story.

Doing Better Than Your Best

During my NYSC program, I taught science courses at Amassoma Grammar School, Bayelsa State. I enjoyed teaching there; I viewed it as an opportunity to mentor teens and youths. I was assigned to teach chemistry and physics. I also volunteered to solve mathematics problems with the students. During my teaching sessions, I always used the opportunity to inspire the students about the importance of education in their future achievements in life and career. I like to do this exercise where I ask the students to close their eyes, visualize where they want to be in five years, in ten years, and so on. I used to tell them my story, how education had changed my world. I used to tell them that education can do the same for them. I encouraged them not to depend on their parents' riches but to work towards a successful academic life. As they closed their eyes, I asked those who wanted to become a fisherman in five years to raise their hands, and one person raised his hand. I asked who would like to gain admission to the university to become a doctor, and many raised their hands... lawyer, engineer, and again many raised their hand. I asked them to open their eyes and congratulated them for going through what I call the mental picture of where you will be in the future.

I urged them to begin to live each day in ways that contributed to becoming the person they wanted to be in the future. I used to tell them: *"When you are about to make a decision to pay attention in class or to get distracted by chatting with your friends at the back of the class, ask yourself which activity can help you towards achieving your goal of becoming an engineer, lawyer, or whatever you have chosen to become."*

I also advised those who want to become fishermen or boat operators to dream higher. If you must be a fisherman, then you can become the best fisherman in town. If you must be a boat operator, then dream to one day become the captain of the damn best ship in the ocean. Someone has to be the captain of the numerous cruise ships we have sailing the oceans today. Do not just set your eyes on the same waters that your father or uncles have fished in all their lives. Branch out, step out, and be different. I presented inspirational stories every now and then to motivate the students and help them understand the importance of education. Essentially, I wanted them to understand that education is meant for their personal development and success, not that of their parents. One day, after delivering my short inspirational message, the class was quiet. I asked if anyone had a question, and I was glad when "Prieye" raised his hand. Prieye happened to be one of the students who paid really good attention in class, and it always seems that there was something holding him back from reaching his true potential.

I was surprised when he uttered his question, *"Sir, are you from a royal family?"* I was not expecting that line of question or reasoning at all. What made him think that education is for the rich, for only people of royal class? Was my story too good to be true? I retold my story to them, how both of my parents were teachers, and how I lost my dad at a young age; how mother promised to ensure that everyone got a minimum of a university degree because she knew the importance of education. I also informed them of the things I had to do to raise money for my education, how I taught in private schools, hawked goods at the motor park, worked in a manufacturing industry, and did quite a number of labor intensive jobs because all served as a means to an end. They all listened with amazement, and I believe some students made important life decisions that day that will help them realize their glorious destiny, while some probably did not. They just enjoyed the story and moved on. They did not believe that an affluent life, a life better than what their parents had to offer, is for them. Just like those students, the decisions you make from the nuggets garnered from this book can impact your life.

Another interesting event happened while I was teaching in a private school during one of my long vacations. I was already a sophomore in college then, and we had about four months of break. I went back to the school where I taught for about a year prior to gaining admission into FUTO. One day as I took a few minutes to speak to the students on the importance of education, I did my regular visualization exercise with the kids. These were primary six students who were getting ready for their secondary school common entrance examinations.

In the middle of the exercise, as I gave advice to the students, one of the kids, who happened to be my name sake, Chinenye, raised his hand to ask a question. He made this announcement to the class with an innocent smile plastered on his face: *"Uncle is using style to preach to us,"* he sheepishly commented. But boy was he right. Indeed I was using the opportunity to inspire them. I wanted them to know that who they become tomorrow will be determined by the decisions and the actions they make and take respectively, today. I told them that when they are doing their homework, they are not doing it for their parents; rather, they are developing their intellect in order to become engineers, doctors, lawyers, accountants, and what have you in the near future. I encouraged them to stay focused with their studies and not to allow anyone to distract them from achieving excellent grades, even when they go to college. I emphasized the difference between people in low skilled labor force jobs (bus conductors and taxi drivers) and people in the high skilled labor force (engineers, doctors, lawyers, accountants, etc.). I tried to instill in them that the decisions they make today will determine which group they will join in the near future. I was not necessarily asking the students to repent and accept Christ or preaching the gospel to the class, but I was inspiring them and coaching them for the life that awaits them in the future. So to an extent, I was not surprised when Chinenye raised his hand and made that comment. I smiled.

On another occasion, I had a parent grant me permission to punish his son if he kept failing or failed to do his homework. I was not used to that, being the kind of teacher you will consider understanding and considerate, not teacher Chike, the type students feared as he approached. I was someone they could run to and relate to with their problems. But for this kid, because of the approval I got from the dad, he received a punishment for any missed score in his homework.

The idea was to help him focus on his studies. He needed any help he could get to solve his problems. This was designed to motivate him to seek help in completing his homework. So any failure meant he was getting punished. Boy, this guy kept failing and having so many poor grades that I could not keep track of the number of punishments that I gave him. It got to a point that a mere look at him brought shudders to his shoulders. I had to rethink my strategy, so I reduced my punishments for not completing his homework. He had become scared of going to school. The parents noticed. If they had not given their permission, this situation could have been bad. To cut the story short, the boy became a good friend of mine in the class. He dreaded coming to school, and the parents also asked me to reduce my punishment, so that was exactly what I did.

I began to sit beside him during class, help him where he had questions and ensuring he understood what to do for his homework. If it meant going through it with him before he left for the day, I did just that. And he started doing better in class. I do not know where he is today. I do not know what he thinks of me or what worked better for him, the mean teacher or the friendly teacher that helped him do his work. If I were in his shoes, I would choose the friendly teacher. Subsequently, I have had opportunities to be a teacher and tutor students, and I usually apply the friendly approach as I understand that people are different. Everyone does not catch on to things as easily as others. You need to understand what works for people. For some people you may need to explain stuff once and they get it. EUREKA! And for others, you may need to explain yourself a couple of times or maybe even use a different description for them to get you.

While I worked at the private school during my holidays, I always gave my 100 percent. This has always been one of my life philosophies; when working at an establishment, treat the company as your own. If you are the director of that company, then you would want for it to succeed, so what are the things that you will do to ensure that the company attains success? Are these things within my jurisdiction to do? If they are, I will do them to the best of my knowledge. I love to treat my work place as my own because I believe in the word of God that states, "And if ye have not been faithful in that which is another man's, who shall give you that which is your own?" —i.e., if you are faithful in that which is another's, God will give you your own. I was first introduced to this passage by Mrs. Ndudi, the director of Divine Will Schools Abayi, the private school that I taught in prior to my college admission. I heard this over and over again, as she repeated a teaching on it every time we had a staff meeting. "And if ye have not been faithful in that which is another man's, who shall give you that which is your own?"[22]— It stuck in my head. I could not live otherwise. She never failed to mention this part of Scripture and what it meant in her life whenever we had a staff meeting. If you are someone who dreams of attaining success like she did, you cannot help but listen to her story and be inspired. You do not necessarily have to become a school director, but you will end well. There will be light for you at the end of the tunnel. You will look back and be able to share the same testimony with friends and relatives as I am doing now. Friends, they say the secret of great men lies in their stories. When you hear it, understand it, and run with it, God will bless the works of your hand. This could be in the area of relationships, career, business, other people's children, church activities, friends, courtship, and all the aspects that make up life.

On Advising People

Many years ago as I packed my luggage at home in Nigeria and looked forward to the trip that would bring me to the United States of America, I was filled with mixed feelings because the next day I would be leaving family and friends behind to travel to a strange land, a land of opportunity, as I had been made to understand.

---

22 Luke 16:12

As the sun was beginning to set, a few people who knew of my impending trip stopped by to either congratulate me or render advice or, better yet, to do both.

"I believe in you; I know what you can do and what you can't do," mother told me. "If someone calls me tomorrow and says that you did this or that, I can defend you and say that you did this or that. I can defend you and say that you got the wrong guy. Chinenye can't do that; I can't picture my son doing that." These were Mother's words as she advised me the night before I left my home country, Nigeria, for a two-year graduate study program in Alaska, USA. The few people who knew that I was leaving the country had similar advice for me; they did not have much to say. All I kept hearing was keep up the good work, you are doing so well, you are a role model to many of our youths. More importantly, most of them prayed for me. I recall the prayer by Mama D:

"May the Lord keep and guide you, you shall eat the good of America," were the last words of Mama D's prayer as she blessed me.

One piece of advice that I did not take very well was from one of my brothers, who was advising me based on the experiences he had heard of. Over and over again, he told me stories of people who got ruined after they went abroad, from stories of men who got carried away with strange women and forgot where they came from, to stories of men and women who tried to hit it quick by taking the fast lane and ended up in trouble. He was asking me not to be like them, not to try to hit it quickly, to take my time and focus on my academics. I was boiling inside while he was giving me this advice and telling me all these weird stories of disappointments that others had experienced. I felt insulted; he should have known better. After all I had been through, did my brother really think of me that way? Is this all he thought of me, as someone that would get carried away by the looseness of women in a strange country? What happened to advice such as be of good cheer; look out for a local church, and be part of it? Do not forget your godly and good heritage. Know that it is God who has brought you this far; do not forsake Him. This is an open door for you…but no, he did not. He was focused on the negatives, and he lost me. I was hurt. As a matter of fact, I walked out as he was making his closing remarks during our family meeting that fateful night.

A similar event happened one day when I received a call from a very good friend of mine, a beautiful lady who caught my attention with her love for God and gentleness. After I informed her of my NYSC posting to Bayelsa State, she proceeded to give me the kind of advice that I did not even get from my mother. She told me about all the women that I was going to be meeting in camp and how I should not get carried away with what they would offer me and all sorts of motherly advice. I listened to her, but then just like I explained earlier about my brother's advice, I was burning inside. I did not take it lightly with her. I directly told her that I did not like her tone of advice. I expected her to believe in me, and this meant she did not understand my stand with God or she just felt that I was going to fall for the first girl that ran into my arms. Not that I had fallen into hers; if I was going to, I lost it at the heels of that advice.

The way you advise people matters. Appreciate the good in them, and do not just focus on the negatives or other people's experiences. In retrospect, I feel it was my sense of pride that caused me to feel that way. I felt I was doing so well as a born again Christian who was committed and devoted to serving God with all that I am and all that I had, including my finances. At that point I had not even kissed a girl, forget about sleeping with one! I planned on marrying that way, just as a way to respect the lady that would be my wife for the rest of my life. My saying then was that I was going to learn the act of love making along with my wife—we would have the same level of experience. Hopefully, that helps you understand where I was coming from, but still today I look back and feel that I was wrong. It was a show of pride. The scripture said, "Let him who thinks he stands take heed, lest he falls."[23] Today I take every bit of advice I get, sieve it through God's word, pray, and trust God to order my steps. I believe in divine direction; it makes life easy. With divine direction, you work in God's favor, and you easily get what others have to struggle to accomplish.

---

[23] See 1 Corinthians 10:12

Chapter  08

Exceeding Expectations

"Whatever your life's work is, do it well. A man should do his job so well that the living, the dead, and the unborn could do it no better." Martin Luther King, Jr.[24]

As a company employee, it is my duty to get the job done. I consider every day at my job as a work interview for my next career move. You can never tell where things will go. Ask Eva in the movie *Deliver Us from Eva*.[25] In this movie, Gabrielle Union, acting as a health inspector named Eva, resisted all attempts by the manager of a high profile restaurant to get her to amend her report. Eva stood her ground. And as the movie progressed, she discovered that the manager

---

24 Martin Luther King, Jr. (January 15, 1929 – April 4, 1968) was an American pastor, activist, humanitarian, and leader in the African-American Civil Rights Movement. He is best known for his role in the advancement of civil rights using nonviolent civil disobedience based on his Christian beliefs.

25 *Deliver Us from Eva* is a 2003 American feature film starring LL Cool J and Gabrielle Union.

who had debated with her, who tried his best to give her reasons to consider amending her report, was actually acting that role. He was there only to witness her work ethics in order to offer her a better job in the city. After she realized what had transpired, she bowed her head and smiled. It was easy for her to smile because this was a positive outcome. As we go about our job responsibilities each day, let's always strive to be the type of employee that any employer simply cannot afford to lose. A good way to achieve this is to establish a track record of high performance by consistently exceeding expectations.

What does it take to exceed expectations at your job? What does it take to be exceptional in executing your responsibilities? Let me answer by drawing from my career experience. To exceed expectations, you have to do more than your assigned job responsibility. You have to do more than showing up at 8:00 a.m. and leaving at 5:00 p.m. because it is when people go home from work. To exceed expectations, you have to do something outside your regular work duties. If you are just doing your assigned duty, you are meeting expectations, but you are not exceeding them, no matter how good you are at doing your job. This became very clear to me during our annual performance review. I received an email from my team leader requesting each of us to send him a list of our accomplishments for the past year. He specifically requested us to list what we had accomplished outside our regular scope of work. In a way, he was looking for what to use to differentiate us from our peers. When I saw this mail, I breathed in and out as I thought of what I had done the past year that was outside my job routine. It was not too difficult a task for me because I was able to list a couple of activities that I had been involved with in the past year. Notable among them was being a lead author and presenter for a conference paper. This paper was later selected and published in the *Journal of Petroleum Technology*. It was a paper I co-authored with my senior work colleagues. Everyone was excited about the publication and the fact the industry recognized our strategic production optimization methodologies that were showcased in the paper.

The other extracurricular activity that I listed was in response to my regional president's request for teams to submit our exemplary efforts to be considered for my company's global award recognition. It was a duty outside my normal work routine. It takes a lot of personal time to be able to use a limited amount of words to present or highlight the challenge that your team faced, the methodology applied to solve the problem, and the results that were achieved. In your report, you also have to be mindful to showcase the impact of the project in delivering value to the company. A lot of people do not usually look into making these entries because of the time commitment that is involved. That year, I led the efforts to put an entry together, and my senior colleagues helped edit the write up to get it to the final submission state. I made the entry submission, and I and every other person who made a submission were recognized by the leadership team for making an effort to showcase the good efforts we were putting in to deliver value to the company. I believe these two activities outside my work routine and delivering on my daily job responsibility led to me receiving an "Exceed Expectation" award for that year. It pays to broadcast your success stories in your job. It makes you visible. Ensure that the work you are doing is visible; if all you do is hidden, no one will know. I am not good at this, so technical paper publishing, in-house or via the Society of Petroleum Engineers (SPE) conferences, is a good way for me to showcase my efforts. Broadcast your success stories; you get recognized when you do.

Another annual performance review in which I also received an exceeded expectations rating came after I volunteered to be one of the people working at locations to help the clean-up efforts after the explosion of an exploratory rig in the Gulf of Mexico in 2010.[26] I happened to join my company about five months before the ugly incident that led to the loss of eleven lives and the disastrous oil spill in the Gulf of Mexico. It was a difficult time for the company, and

---

26 Vergano, Dan. Final report finds several faults in Gulf oil spill (December 14, 2011). http://usatoday30.usatoday.com/news/nation/story/2011-12-14/gulf-oil-spill-bp/51928228/1

volunteers were drawn from every part of the world to help with the clean-up efforts. My manager asked if I was willing to join the operations team that was supporting the clean-up efforts. I accepted and was part of the operations team at Venice, Louisiana, for a period of two months. That year, I also served in a leadership capacity as the production engineering discipline representative for the new hire program at my place of work. In this role, you are required to organize seminars, lunch and learn events, site visits to third-party companies, and personal development plan reviews sessions by senior colleagues for new hires in production engineering. This helped me network and build a technical network. Accepting a duty that was not a part of my regular job role set me apart and positioned me to receive an Exceed Expectations award. And I did.

To exceed expectations, go the extra mile, do things faster, and do things with greater sincerity and friendliness for customers, employees, family, and yourself. Be a team player; have the ability to persuade, negotiate, compromise, and make others feel important. If you cannot work well with others, you will not make headway in your career. When you have the right attitude, people will like to work with you. Being a team player is one of the required right attitudes to excel in your workplace. Do not let it always be your way or the highway. Such people do not make it to the top. Concentrate and focus on the task that is assigned to you. Having clarity with your main task and understanding your responsibility is paramount if you are to deliver a track record of high performance and achieve excellent results. It is helpful to know why you are on the payroll. A lot of people leave their job for another job, not because they are not being paid well but because they do not feel fulfilled in their perceived contribution to the company's success. Knowing your role helps you know exactly what is expected of you and how relevant tasks are to be measured. "Good enough" seldom is. An attitude of "that is good enough" will not get you to the top. What is your personal level of excellence? Are you driven? For me, it is my commitment, discipline, and responsibilities that keep me going when the going gets tough.

Training and skill development help you to establish your placement. Your progress requires continuous involvement in skill development and capacity development. It takes skill both to secure and sustain success. You never find a four star general that is not a product of training. Training is also the trade secret of every sports star, i.e., a rigorous commitment to training. Through training, you follow the steps of giants in your field.

Another aspect of exceeding expectations is to meet deadlines. When you cannot meet a particular deadline, explain why you cannot do so, not at the deadline date but prior to the deadline. Discussing the challenges to meeting any deadline with my team leader as they arise helped me in a way because on occasions, he even proffered solutions, offering an easy way out. It is not good practice to surprise your team leader or supervisor at the deadline with challenges you faced that he or she did not know about. Do not show up at the deadline with reasons why you could not get the job done; they will appear to be excuses, especially if these were challenges that your team leader could have helped you get through. Remember, there is a reason why he or she is your team leader. Leaders are there to help you succeed; if you run into challenges on a project, make him or her aware, seek guidance, and give a reason why a certain deadline cannot be met well before the deadline so that it does not appear that you waited until the last minute to discover those challenges, hence you could not meet the deadline. If your team leader and senior work colleagues are kept in the know and they have made their contributions through conversations with you, they will defend you in your absence because they have the information. If they are not aware, they will just say, "I don't really know what's going on; I think he is working on it." Not good.

When your team leader is looking for someone to help with a new project, no it is not part of your work plan, but go ahead and take the additional responsibility. It might require you to add a few extra hours of work a day for a period of time, but you are setting yourself up to exceed expectations. When your team leader is asking this at a team meeting, he/she knows those who can do it and the people with a bit of free space to do it, and she can easily assign it to them, but if you have free space and do not accept it and someone else who does not have as much space as you accepts it, you are setting yourself up for failure. I hate it when people say, "I'm looking out for me; I will only perform the duties I have been assigned, duties I'm being paid for. I am not volunteering for more projects. Pay me more if you want more from me." That will only lead to a mediocre life. You cannot exceed expectations by meeting expectations. You cannot exceed expectation by only delivering on your assigned responsibilities.

As a factory worker in Luscana Nigeria Limited, a shoe manufacturing plant, in 1997, right after I graduated from high school, I did more than exceed expectations. To start with, I went the whole nine yards to get this job. This was one job I was consistently told that I was overqualified for. The company prefers to recruit high school drop outs or people who did not make it through school. They did this because their retention rate was high. They view people like me as using them to while away time until we got admission to higher institutions or universities. Looking back now I think their philosophy was good as a business decision. Another reason why they could have turned me down on several occasions was that I was just 16 years old at the time of my application. I wanted this job even though I knew it was not the best job for me, but it was right there across the road from where my family lived.

I had to go with my mum who talked the personnel manager into considering my application. That day, after five tries, one with my mother, he gave me a job as a machine operator. I was recruited into the factory during same period that another young high school graduate, Bethel, was to begin employment. Fascinated by the manufacturing process that was being employed at this factory, I looked forward to going to work each day. We were using an extrusion process to manufacture studs, men's and ladies rubber sandals and shoes, flat soles for sandals, etc. We had two grinding machines that we used to recycle worn out rubber materials such as old shoes and sandals. After grinding them, they are sieved to eliminate dust and solids that could affect the quality of the final product. Several chemicals are then applied as the cut rubber materials are heated up in a warm oven, far below the melting point of rubber materials. One of the chemicals, a yellow product, was used to add smoothness and shine to the finished product. Another chemical, we called it the white one, performed the same action that yeast does on flour in the bread manufacturing process. So it was critical that both chemicals were added in the right proportion for good quality control. A mere visual observation of the product could tell if the yellow chemical was added in the right proportion. On the other hand, the weight of a well optimized fill for a rubber shoe sole will speak of the proportion of white chemical that had been added. These are usually roles assigned to the shift supervisors.

Another important role assigned to the shift leads was to optimize the injection feed into the modules and ensure that the right shoe sizes, per demand, were manufactured by monitoring the output and the molds that were active in the system. I was not a shift lead, but it did not take me long to understand the system and to understand how the machine worked and what the machine responded to. I watched the lead technicians make changes to the machine using radio buttons on the control panel whenever they wanted to optimize the system. I asked questions, and they answered the ones they knew. When I tried to enquire further, I was shocked when I was told that they really did not know the details. They were just going with the flow; that was how it has been, that was what the manager wanted them to do, and it had always worked, so if it is not broken, do not fix it.

Being the curious type, I continued to monitor the response by the machine as they made their changes to the system; with time, I began to see the answers to my questions. I could connect the dots.

So when there was a system upset and the lead technician wanted to make changes to the system, I voluntarily told him what to do, especially if I thought that what he was about to do would not fix the issue. When they noticed that my suggestions were working, they formed a habit of requesting my opinion and thoughts on what to do when a system misbehaved. As a matter of fact, I was given a new name. One day, my factory manager recognized my efforts in troubleshooting the machines' manufacturing process and my ability to speak out to ensure that we were optimizing the manufacturing process properly. He called me an academic operator. They asked me what I was going to study in school; I told them that I planned to become an engineer. This was one of the experiences that enhanced my vision of joining the engineering profession.

One notable change that I implemented at the company occurred when the company reinstated one of its machines that had been unused for a couple of years. The new machine used the same manufacturing process as the one that had been in operation but looked different. It so happened that all the molds where either being half filled or overfilled during the manufacturing process. All kinds of troubleshooting was done but to no avail. On my own, without any request from anyone, and from what I must have learned from operating the other machinery, I noticed that the molds were being fed by different settings on the control panel. You see, whenever a mold gets under the extrusion point of the machine, the screw inside the system rotates and carries material into the filling chamber of the machinery. Depending on the set point, which is based on the size of the sole or rubber sandals being manufactured, it stops, carries the mold up to the injection point and the mold is filled with molten rubber material.

The molten rubber materials cools, solidifies, and takes the shape and size of the mold. I noticed that when mold number 5 was getting ready to be filled, it was mold number 7 control that was lit on the control board. Hence, if I kept adjusting mold number 5 setting on the control panel to match reality, I would keep being off, because that number 5 was being used to feed a different mold, maybe mold number 3. That explained why a mold would fill correctly in one round and by the next round it would either be overfilled or cut short due to inadequate fill. I caught this and began to change the settings myself; before anyone could tell what was going on, all the soles and shoes were coming out in the right proportions, just the way we wanted them to. I explained the process to my manager, and he once again called me an academic operator. He said that I would make an excellent engineer and thanked me for exceeding expectations. My manager was so happy that apart from giving me a financial bonus, he also made me a special operator. Whenever this machine was in operation, I was made to sit beside the control panel to optimize the system as necessary. This taught me the import of paying attention to details.

Another time I paid this much attention to details happened when I worked as an office assistant at the conference services department of the University of Alaska Fairbanks. I worked over the summer with conference services department of residence life, University of Alaska Fairbanks. My direct supervisor, Mrs. Amber, doubled as the marketing manager for the department, so she gave me that year's student exit survey to key in into the departments database. While doing this, I came across a folder that contained the analyzed data for the exit and room selection survey for the past year. I noticed their interpretation of the data, so I went ahead to analyze the current years data and prepared the annual report in colorful pie charts, histograms, and tables. When I presented the work to my supervisor, she was so pleased. Voluntarily, I had done more than was required of me. She recognized my efforts with an employee of the month award and with two free movie tickets and other benefits.

My unwavering pursuit of excellence motivates me greatly. I have always been motivated by the desire to do a good job at whatever position I am in. I want to excel and to be successful in my job, both for my own personal satisfaction and for my employer. One thing I love so much is facing new challenges and going the extra mile. This attribute is needed in your journey to become the type of employee that any employer simply cannot afford to lose.

Chapter 09

PetroBowl Champions

"One of the greatest discoveries a man makes, one of his greatest surprises, is to find he can do what he was afraid he couldn't." - Henry Ford[27]

There is a famous saying that says, "Fear is faith that something won't work out." Most people believe their doubts and doubt their belief. Worry is a route that leads from somewhere to nowhere; never let it direct your life. Your life will expand or shrink in proportion to what you think is possible. Dare to think unthinkable thoughts; you never know what you cannot do until you try. Truthfully, Richard DeVos stated and I quote, "The only thing that stands between a man and what he wants from life is often merely the will to try it and the faith to believe that it is possible."[28] The famous American

---

27 Henry Ford (July 30, 1863 – April 7, 1947) was an American industrialist, the founder of the Ford Motor Company, and sponsor of the development of the assembly line technique of mass production.
28 DeVos, Richard and Conn, Charles Paul. Believe! Berkley. Revised Edition (May 1, 1985).

industrialist Henry Ford said, "One of the greatest discoveries a man makes, one of his greatest surprises, is to find he can do what he was afraid he couldn't." Indeed, fear could keep you from going where you could have won. The first time I heard this statement, it was at a Lakewood Church service in Houston, Texas. It took me down memory lane.

In 2007 and 2008 I represented the University of Oklahoma student chapter of the Society of Petroleum Engineers (SPE) in the annual PetroBowl international competition hosted each year by the young professionals at the society's Annual Technical Conference and Exhibitions (ATCE) event. Both years, we were crowned champions. Prior to that, in 2003, I had declined an opportunity to represent my school in a similar competition in my home country, Nigeria, only to realize, while sitting down in the audience, that I could have answered all the technical questions meant for the contestants. I felt miserable.

Many years later, at a regular Sunday service at Lakewood Church, I heard the pastor state that "Fear can stop you from going where you could have won." I understood him completely. Without doubt, my mind went to my PetroBowl experience. Lakewood is a dynamic church in the heart of Houston, led by Pastor Joel Osteen, and it currently has the biggest church auditorium in the United States. When Pastor Joel Osteen made that statement, it took me down memory lane. I thought of the PetroBowl competition that was held at Nicon Hilton Hotel in Abuja, Nigeria, in 2003. This was a competition amongst the student chapters of the society of petroleum engineers in Nigeria. As an outstanding final year student, actually the best student in the petroleum engineering department, everyone nominated me and the then secretary general of our student chapter (FUTO) to represent my school at the competition. Their belief was that Excel and Austin were their best chance at winning the competition. I was okay with the plan. I was to cover technical questions while my colleague, Austin, the student chapter secretary, who happens to also be the best in his class, would have to cover current affairs in the oil and gas industry.

However, on the day of the event, as time for the event approached, the organizers chose to have only one student represent each school. Each school was required to select one student to represent them in the competition. That is when I allowed fear to creep into my mind and stop me from going where I could have won. I was asked to represent my school, but I recalled the experience I had in the regional competition. A couple of months before the national competition, I was nominated to represent my school in the regional competition hosted by the SPE student chapter in my alma mater. I gladly accepted, after being promised that only petroleum engineering technical questions would be asked. Because the questions were set by the current SPE student leadership in my school, I believed them. I had no idea what the questions involved, but I believed that it would be relating to the petroleum engineering industry, and with my experience in the industry, I was confident of doing a good job and hopefully winning the competition for my school. When the competition commenced, the moderator informed us that we had about 20 questions to choose from. As he got to your turn, you are required to choose a number between one and 20 for the question you want to answer, and he would read out the question to you.

The first student to answer was a student from the University of Port Harcourt, and he chose question number one. The question was "Who is the current minister of petroleum resources for Nigeria?" I did not recall if he got the question right or wrong, but I could not help but think of what my own question could be. To me, this kind of question was not the typical oil and gas industry question that I was expecting. I expected technical questions. Next in line was a student from the Rivers State University of Science and Technology. He picked question number seven, and it read, "Who is the current CEO of Shell Petroleum Development Company of Nigeria Limited?" Your guess is as good as mine on where my thoughts were going at this point. The hall was full of FUTO students. Then it was my turn, and I picked question number five. The question was "How many refineries do we have in Nigeria, and what are the three cities where they are located?" Ah, this is it?

After a bit cracking of my head and hearing people whisper the answer from the audience, I was able to assay that we had four refineries in Nigeria located in Warri, Kaduna, and Port Harcourt. We have two in Port Harcourt. The students clapped; I got one more question right, and that was it. I felt miserable, like a failure. There were many students in the audience that could have done far better than my performance if they had the opportunity. I was relying on answering technical questions, but most of the questions were about CEOs of multinational organizations, the current president of OPEC, the chairman of NNPC, and other current affairs questions that relate to the oil and gas sector in Nigeria. I was not cut out or prepared for that; no one told me to expect current affairs questions. It was a last minute change by the SPE leadership to make it a neutral competition, as the question was being set by students from one institution. I was not informed so that I would not have an advantage over contestants from other institutions. If I was informed, I would have asked for a different student to represent us or at least do a little research to get myself ready for the competition. I am a very competitive person, so not being prepared is not my kind of situation.

The experience and the fear of failing again caused me to decline the opportunity to represent my school in the national competition that year. Instead, I nominated my colleague who was a year below me, and, at the time, the SPE student chapter secretary general. My thought was that he presented the best opportunity for us to win. That was the argument, my argument that helped convince everyone to allow Austin to be our sole representative in the competition. He did well; he took the third position. A student from Petroleum Training Institute took first place. What pained me was that this time it was all technical questions in petroleum engineering. I could answer all the questions while sitting with the audience. I felt horrible. I was rightly informed that this time it was going to be all technical questions, but fear of the past events did not allow me to believe them. In fact, I convinced my school colleagues that even if it was all technical, Austin was a smart student who could pull through. So when I was seated with the audience, I was giving the answers before the contestants could answer them, and students sitting around me, even students from other schools, began to ask, "Why are you not representing your school? You seem to know it all. If you know this much, why are you not up there?" I felt bad, and at that very moment, I made a decision never to give up an opportunity again due to my past performance. I chose to believe in myself again and never allow my history (my yesterday) to kill my destiny (my tremendous future). I was determined to make amends. And make amends I did when I got an opportunity to represent my school, the University of Oklahoma (OU), in the same competition, but this time at the international stage.

My first time witnessing the international competition was in 2006 at the Colorado Convention Centre in Denver. Sitting as a member of the audience, I watched my school's team lose to the eventual champions, Colorado School of Mines, in the semi-finals of the competition. The OU team jumped to an early lead in the first half of the semi-finals only to lose out by a margin in the second half. Again, I was busy whispering answers to the questions for my neighbors, sometimes even before the moderator could completely narrate the questions to the contestants. There and then, I knew that I would do well if I was to be a member of the team.

I vowed to become one and to join the team for next year's competition, and so I did. I attended practice and review sessions for the PetroBowl competition at my school. We had a very dedicated instructor who served as a moderator and helped prepare us for the competition. He did a very good job of compiling questions, oil and gas industry questions, and several questions similar to what is usually posed to contestants at the competition. As a new member who did not have access to the materials, I was participating actively and answering questions, even the new questions that the instructor kept adding each week. It came as no surprise when I got selected as the graduate student representative to be a member of the team. It was a no brainer. We had a team of four: three undergraduate students and one graduate student.

This time, ATCE was being held at the Anaheim Convention Center in Los Angeles, California. I looked forward to not just attending the conference this time but representing my school in the PetroBowl competition. The schedule came out, and we were matched against Texas A&M University (TAMU), our toughest opposition in the competition. I say toughest opponent because we were 10 seconds away from losing to them. With 10 seconds to go, TAMU had 90 points to our 80 points. It was up to us to provide the answer to the next toss up question or go home. It was a tense moment; one of my team members had buzzed in a little too early during the last question and missed out on getting it right.

Luckily for us, the other team could not get the correct answer either. So we remained only 10 points down. When a contestant presses his or her buzzer, the moderator has to stop reading the remaining part of the question, while giving the contestant who buzzed in an opportunity to answer the question. If the contestant fails to answer the question correctly, the other team gets the privilege of hearing the rest of the question and answering. Being smart in this competition requires one to have a foresight or have insight to where the question is going. If you can correctly decipher what the question is going to be before the moderator makes it known to everyone by completely stating the question, and answer it correctly, you win 10 points and an opportunity to win bonus points by answering another question. Also, both teams can wait until the moderator completely describes the question and then if you know the answer, you can buzz in and whoever buzzes in first is allowed to answer and win points for his team. A correct answer gives you another opportunity to win more points by answering a bonus question. The toss-up questions are worth 10 points, while the bonus questions are worth 15 to 30 points.

As the seconds continued to tick and run down, I could see the tension on people's faces. The room was quiet. Apart from the moderator's voice as he read the toss up questions, one could have easily heard the sound of a pin drop. I was tense, but I knew it was no time to be tense. I needed to understand the question so I could answer correctly. I was nervous. I began to pray, oh Lord help me get the answer to the next question. I repeated this prayer over and over again as the moderator narrated the next question. It happened to be a question that required the moderator to narrate the function of an organization, and he only mentioned the acronym of the energy organization. It was the IEA. As he narrated the story, an insight came to me; I guessed that the question was going to be what is the full meaning of IEA, as in what does the acronym IEA stand for?

So I buzzed in before he got to state the question. All eyes were on me. Why did he buzz in? The moderator has not even asked the question. As far as people were concerned, he was just telling a story. Oh, I have buzzed in, now what? Everyone was looking up to me to provide an answer to a question that had not even been asked. I went ahead to provide an answer as my spirit prompted me. I was like, "God, please let this be the answer." My answer was "International Energy Agency". The moderator looked at me, turned to the audience, then looked at the panel of judges, and they gave him a nod.

Then I knew I gave the correct answer. I had offered the correct answer to an unknown question. The moderator declared, "That's correct," and the hall went agog. OU fans shouted and began jumping up and down, shouting and singing. That gave us 10 points and equalized the scores. We went ahead to answer the bonus question and won the game as time ran out before the moderator could complete the next toss up question. We had won! Shouts of "Boomer Sooner" erupted in every part of the room. It is amazing what victory can do to a group; the students from the school that lost narrowly were still seated, probably mourning over what could have been. The once quiet hall could no longer contain the noise that ensued, it had to send some to neighboring halls and walkways. People came and hugged us, mostly OU students and Nigerians who knew me. OU students congratulated us for defeating the Texas A&M Aggies.

My instructor called for our attention though; he begged us not to keep it that close again. In his words, "I almost had a heart attack." We seem to have granted him his request because the next opponent we met we beat 220 to 20 points. As an OU student put it, we lapped them. The score board was not set up to get up to 200, so when we passed 200 points, the system reset our score of 220 to 20 points. So it was as if we had equal scores, but as I stated earlier, we lapped them. That is a funny way to put it. I answered a lot of questions during the second round. I was riding the momentum of the last competition. I was flowing in a way that I was not allowing the moderator to complete the questions before buzzing in to answer. I did this so much that people called the round a one man's show by Excel. It felt good because though I was buzzing in before the moderator completed each question, I got the answers right. We went ahead to defeat other top schools on our way to winning the PetroBowl competition in 2007 and successfully defending the trophy in 2008 as a member of a different OU PetroBowl team. It was a first win for OU at the PetroBowl competition, and the news went far and wide.

I was so excited to have defeated the University of Texas Longhorns in the final round of both competitions because this was a school I applied to that could not make provision for my admission into their PhD program. It was payback, and my team helped me beat them two times in a row, both in the final rounds. I was glad, and I did tell one of their professors when I got the opportunity to chat with her. The story of our championship was circulated to alumni, and we even got rewards from some of them. Notable among them was the chief financier of the department, Engr. Mewbourne, who offered to match the financial award of $2,500 that was given to us by the PetroBowl organizers. We also received college football tickets to the Sooners game against Texas Christian University (TCU) from the dean of my college.

It is good to differentiate between bad fear and good fear. You see, bad fear does not get you out of trouble; it gets you into trouble. Good fear keeps you away from trouble, e.g., when a car is coming your way at great speed, something makes you get out of the way to stay alive for the people who love you. Fear gives you a negative outlook of the future, a negative outlook of what the future holds. Think the right thoughts. Perfect love casts out fear; do not let the devil sneak in and lure you into making a decision based on fear or your emotions. No decision made by bad fear turns out good.

The more you feed the monster, the bigger it gets. Just because I feel it does not mean it is right. Just because it is real does not mean it is right. What you are facing is real, but it may not be right. The more you turn to God for what to do, the better your life gets. Do not respond to the experiences of life with emotion, especially when your emotions are not aligned with the word of God. If you are afraid to fly, fly more often; by the time you fly 100 times, you will be sleeping on the plane, even in turbulent flights. One of the preachers I respect, Pastor Matthew Ashimolowo,[29] once shared a story about how he was frightened about the instability of their plane during his flight to London until the Syrian lady beside him tapped his shoulder and requested him to wake her up when they got to London. Wow, and the man of God was busy praying in tongues, blaming the devil for plane instability and turbulent conditions in the air.

That was a long time ago; he is well accustomed to flying now. I do not blame him though; I can relate to his experience. I used to be just like him. I love travelling, but I dread plane instability and turbulent conditions. I also do not like the pressure changes that

---

29 Matthew Ashimolowo is the Senior Pastor of Kingsway International Christian Centre in London.

occur during take-off and landing. Something in my head does not like it. I usually hold tight to my seat, as if it helps the plane in any way. When the plane is taking off or landing, there is always this priceless expression on my face that says, get it over with already. I used to fast and pray before taking a flight, all because of the fear of all that could go wrong.

Do I do the same for driving around the city? No. And yet anything could happen just driving to the grocery store or taking a trip downtown. I have seen a ghastly motor accident occur on my way to work at an inner city intersection. This is the last place you will expect a motor accident to ever occur, but it so happened that there was a local police chase to arrest a drunk lady. The lady was trying to escape the police, ran a red light, and collided with another vehicle and the driver of that vehicle, who was on his way to work at 7:00 a.m. in the morning and was pronounced dead on the spot. This event happened less than 15 minutes before I left my home that day to cross this intersection. For some reason I was late leaving my home that day and so stayed away from the road as the event unfolded. God has ways of protecting His own.

Now back to my flight adventures. I have flown so many times because my job requires me to travel often that rather than get scared of flights, I actually look forward to it. There is something about reading a book 36,000 feet above sea level or just catching a nap or getting some sleep on the plane.

Friends, fear is not of God. The Bible states that God has not given us the spirit of fear, but of love, of power, and of a sound mind.[30] I knew this, but still, every time I travelled, I had this terrible fear that something bad was going to happen. Each time I flew, I had this phobia that the plane's engines were going to develop a mechanical problem or failure and we were going to take a deep dive and free fall to the earth. But studying God's word removed that fear in me.

---

30 1 Timothy 2: 7

Studying God's word allowed His truth to dwell richly in me so that when fear rears its ugly head in my mind, there is always a word to kill it. It is a battle of the mind. I knew that if I could win the battle in the mind, I would live a happy life. I committed to a life above fear. Studying the word of God grew my faith. I replaced my fear with faith. The Bible says[31] that faith comes by hearing and hearing by the word of God. The scripture that ministered greatly to me was Psalm 91. I consistently reminded myself that I am not going anywhere until I have fulfilled the assignment that He gave me. I read this scripture every time I was travelling until I practically could recite it by heart. Today, I believe so much in those scriptures that I no longer have any form of fear about travelling. In fact, I could sleep through a turbulent flight.

This came in handy when I worked in Wyoming and had to travel to Houston, Texas, almost every month for business meetings or training. Please understand that you have to fly a small plane from Rock Springs, Wyoming, to Denver, Colorado—A not-so-smooth flight that many people will choose to take a five-hour drive to Denver or three-hour drive to Salt Lake City in order to avoid. In 2012, when I was about to book my last flight for a trip to Wyoming, one of my colleagues informed me that there was a plane crash involving that small airport every decade and that this year was the tenth anniversary of the last plane crash that involved that airport.

Talk about adding gasoline to fire! Almost all of my colleagues booked flights to Salt Lake City (SLC) Airport in Utah, and this probably had more to do with the scary nature of flying the small plane from Denver to Rock Springs (RKS) airport than the potential of the plane crashing on the tenth anniversary of doom. The story helped make the decision a no brainer for some people. It was different for me. I know the Lord I serve, and my heart was settled. I am not going anywhere until I have completed my assignment here

---

31 Romans 10:17

on earth, which He has placed in my heart. I went ahead to book my flight for the Rock Springs municipal airport, and you know what, those flights on that last trip were the smoothest I ever experienced of the 40 or more times that I have flown in small planes.

God's word says that I shall not die but live to declare the goodness of the Lord.[32] His word says that He has a plan for my life, a plan to give me a future and a hope.[33] On a fateful day, on a flight from Denver, Colorado, to Houston, 36,000 feet up in the sky, I was reading Kenneth Hagin's book *Plans Purposes & Pursuits*.[34] And reading it, I realized a lot. You can achieve so much in five minutes working on God's plan than you will achieve in five years working on your own plan. When we pursue God's purpose rather than our own, the Holy Spirit is free to move in our midst. He can accomplish more in five minutes than we could accomplish in five years. You do not do something because someone else is doing it. Find out what God wants you to do, and stick to it. Are you willing to pay the price to go further with God?

4 on 4 Basketball

On April 22, 2011, I played a four on four half-court basketball game and made the winning three point shot, while everyone shouted the loudest "no" ever addressed or directed to me as an individual. "Don't shoot! No!" everyone shouted as I went up to take a shot at netting the three ball. I got that response because of all the misses I had made near the rim as the game progressed. Even my opponents joined the chorus, out of natural pity. He stopped defending me and asked me not to shoot because I would not make it. No one believed I could make the winning shot, not even my opponents. But going against expectations on the spur of the moment, I did; and you know what,

---

32 Psalm 118:17
33 Jeremiah 29:11
34 Haggin, Kenneth. Plans Purposes & Pursuits, Faith Library Publications (August 1, 1988)

they were all jubilant. What a shot, was everyone's response. They all came over and gave me high fives. They shared in the joy they could not cheer me up to attain. Friends, I tell you, if you refuse to be distracted, your detractors will soon be attracted. Your detractors will always join to celebrate when you win. Let their detraction spur you to take that winning shot.

Chapter **10**

Money Matters

"And if you have not been faithful in what is another man's, who will give you what is your own?"[35]

As a kid, I was taught that you do not appear before God empty. Before we left for church, my parents always gave my siblings and me an offering for the day. On thanksgiving days, we received two offerings. At first, being a kid, I did it because everyone was doing it. Any kid who did not have an offering ran to their parents to get one. It was instilled in me that it was the right thing to do. It was a popular saying that when you give to God, He will multiply it in ten or hundred folds return. We gave every Sunday and at mid-week services, but as a child, I never really tried to find out how we get these returns, because on the next Sunday, I would be looking up to

---

35 Luke 16:12

my parents for another offering. What I did not realize was that I was sowing for my future.

My pastor ministered about it one day; "Givers never lack" was the title of his message. Do not allow your current conditions to stop you from giving; in fact, give more when what you have is not big enough to solve your financial problems. I believe it was after I joined the Living Faith Church that I began to channel all that I had, all my pocket money, to ensure that I did not appear before God empty. I budgeted my finances to ensure that if I was going to attend the three services we had each week, I would not appear before God empty. I always had something to give.

Sometimes, during my teenage days, I would have the urge to buy a biscuit or snack with the last cash left in my wallet. It would be so tempting, looking at the ice-cream or snack vendors drive their carts past you. It could be yoghurt, hamburger, gala (beef roll), fish roll, you name it. But then I had to consider it…this could be my offering for the mid-week service; if I use it now, I will not have an offering for service, and I never wanted to appear before God empty. I knew God wanted me to be happy, so sometimes I would just pray and say, *"God, please provide for me so that I will have enough money to buy these snacks and still be able to give offering during the midweek service."*

At times, God answered. One of my siblings would just order the snack that I was praying for on the way home and share with me. We are a close-knit family, so we always liked to share what we had with each other. You see, my relationship with God had grown to a level where out of my affection or love, I give. I am passionate enough to give. It is not dependent on what He has done for me. This is not said to belittle the act of thanksgiving, for I always thank God both by words and by giving thanksgiving offerings whenever He blesses me in any area of my life. Giving a thanksgiving offering every time my examination results came out was a habit. It is easy when you have good results; I would give testimony and give thanksgiving offerings. As time passed by, I began to give a thanksgiving offering after every exam I took because the news of missing scripts was rampant in Nigerian universities. So I gave a thanksgiving offering, thanking God ahead of time and believing He would send His angels to protect my papers and ensure that nothing went wrong at the exam hall, as my answer scripts were being marked, or as my scores were being recorded or transferred to wherever they needed to be recorded.

Certainly, it was obvious to me that if I desired breakthroughs in my personal life, one of the fastest ways of achieving it was to have a strong affection for God and His kingdom. I am a firm believer that kingdom connection rains down favor on you, so much that you will not need to pray for most things before you get them. As Dr. Mike Murdock[36] put it, everything you give to God multiplies, including nothing. As long as you are giving and sowing seeds, you will be blessed and receive your harvest. Givers never lack. It does not matter what religious background you are, you receive your blessings. Even unbelievers receive when they give. Many unbelievers understand this more than Christians; that is why you see them give to charities and help the needy. That is how to multiply. In life, seed time and harvest will never cease. Today, when certain things come easy to me, I do not take it for granted. I just tell myself that is part of my harvest coming to me. Keep sowing; bountiful harvest awaits you in your future. When giving becomes your lifestyle, prosperity becomes your identity and heritage. I pray that you receive the power and giving nature that creates an open heaven.

When you love God, you live according to the scripture that "all things work together for your good."[37] I trust God. I believe that if it happens, it is God, and if it does not happen, it is God. I believe in the saying that the proof of one's love for God is obedience to His word. I express my love towards Him by keeping his commandments. We win God's love by loving Him, and we express our love for Him by keeping His commandments.

---

36 Dr. Michael Murdock is an American televangelist and pastor of the Wisdom Center ministry based in Fort Worth, Texas.
37 Romans 8:28

Another proof of love is giving. My belief in the popular saying that "you can give without loving, but you cannot love without giving" helps me freely give, and not just to friends. I always seek opportunities to give back to my community. I have always been a giver in the Kingdom. I can give 100% of my finances to God. Because all I have belongs to Him, I do not find it difficult to give. I am blessed to be a blessing—that is my mind set. Whether it is by giving to the church, supporting a good cause, paying my tithes, or giving to the poor or needy, I do it with abundance of joy in my heart. More often than not, I pay my tithes to my local church; some other times I give my tithes to people in need be it someone I know, a stranger, or fellow church members. To me, it is also a way to minister to God in tithes and offerings.

Giving brings me joy; in fact, I feel horrible when I do not have to give. I seek opportunities to be a blessing to people's lives. I recall one time when I received my bonus check at the beginning of my career as a petroleum engineer in the oil and gas industry. I had this standing award at my alma mater where I presented an award to the best three freshman students and the best graduating student in the winners campus fellowship. This was an award I received as a freshman member of the Christ ambassadors students outreach (CASOR), so I decided to establish it in winners campus fellowship in the same school. The award was later expanded to all levels and best female and best male graduating students. I was sponsoring these awards even as a graduate student and continue to do so.

One day a member of the fellowship called to inform me that he was having difficulty paying his school fees. I was touched. I also knew that he probably was not the only one that needed help with his school fees, so I asked him to make an announcement at the next fellowship meeting for everyone that had problem with paying their school fees. I asked them to add up the figures and get back to me, and I would see what I could do to raise the money; maybe I could help pay some part of the money for them. When the final figure got to me, I believe it was about three to five students who had not completed their school fees that year. This was in 2010.

When I got the total amount required, I was shocked that it was not as big as I was expecting; I could afford the total amount with what I had in my account. So I sent the money to pay for the remaining school fees for those students, the people who had not paid, and those who requested help, along with financial support for the fellowship and the annual award prize and gifts for the best students. I have said it before and permit me to say it again, when giving becomes your lifestyle, prosperity becomes your heritage. I pray that you receive the power and giving nature that creates an open heaven.

Tithes, Seeds, and Offering

Believe it or not, your decisions are going to determine how successful you are in life. There are certain choices that greatly affect your life. The choices you make concerning your career, your soul mate, your friends, and especially your money can greatly determine how far you go in life. I understand that as human beings, we are free moral agents, and my life is on the line when I make decisions. So I always strive to make wise decisions.

Life is a series of decisions. When you wake up in the morning, you are confronted with decisions—whether to lie in bed or get up and take a shower, eat your breakfast or skip it, pray or not say your morning prayers, drive your car to work or take a bus, if you are driving—overtake the old lady driving at 10 mph in front of you or drive gently behind her. To be successful in life is to be a successful decision maker. To make a good decision is to make a decision that takes you towards fulfilling your life purpose. Every decision is based on some knowledge, half knowledge, or full knowledge. For me, the final authority in decision making is based on the word of God. Not friends, not CNN, not what the media thinks or says, not my parents, but God's word. If God said it, I believe it, and that settles it.

I think of men of God who made it in the Bible. David gave everything he had towards building God's church.[38] Solomon made so many sacrifices to God that it led to a divine encounter with God.[39] Abraham always paid his tithe.[40] Today we all pray "Abraham's blessings are mine," and I then ask myself, do you not need to do what Abraham did for you to be a candidate to receive Abrahamic blessings? Can God trust you to sacrifice your only son "Isaac"?

Do not rejoice that you have no son called Isaac; your Isaac could be the amount you have in your checking account. It could be your luxurious car. It could be your only car, no matter how rundown it looks. I have heard testimonies about people selling their cars to sow as seeds for the growth of His kingdom and obtaining a great turnaround in the affairs of their life. It could be increasing your tithe to increase your income. How about a seed of your monthly mortgage payment to gain a debt free home? It is to everyone according to your faith. I once emptied my bank account for a good cause, the annual award that I instituted at the campus fellowship in my alma mater.

On my way to send the money, I made a call to get details on whose name (the campus fellowship's treasurer or president) I should use to send the MoneyGram to them only to find out that schools in Nigeria had been closed down for some weeks, hence, the graduation ceremony was going to be on hold until ASUU (an association of academic university staff in Nigeria) ended their strike. It was a big relief; that bought me some time. I had already passed a big test. This led to a very insightful period in my life. I discovered the answer to my simulation hitches, making tremendous headway in my dissertation research. I was ready to graduate, and everything made sense again.

---

38 1 Chronicles 29:2
39 2 Chronicles 1
40 Genesis 14:19-20

Do Not Eat Your Seed

On the afternoon of September 15, 2012, as I watched Jay Austin, a motor car salesman in the movie *Flywheel*[41] discover that his total sales profit was exactly how much he needed to pay back the people he had cheated prior to re-dedicating his life to Christ, I could not help but wonder what he would do. He had two options: consume the seed or invest it by paying back all the people he and his salesmen had cheated. He chose the latter, and when the news broke out that he had not always been honest, it was the people he paid back that came to his defense.

Such stories appeal to me because they are true. They prove that our God is faithful. Think what ruin he would have faced had he not paid back these people. As the story portrayed, paying back some of these people was an answered prayer to them. What has God been asking you to do that you have been holding off on? Who has God been asking you to bless that you have not? Have you been eating your seed instead of investing or sowing them? It is not too late to make amends and to begin to live an honest life, and our good Lord will bless the works of your hand and keep you on the winning lane of life.

For the greater part of year 2002 and early 2003, I lived at my Aunty Nwamaka's place in the garden city of Port Harcourt (PH), not too far from my family home. I was a junior in college, and after the first semester, I was required to complete a six-month engineering internship program. I did not have a placement yet, and I had not even spent a night in PH before then. But Mum made some calls and contacted my aunt, who lived with her family in PH. She knew I was doing well in school, and she gracefully accepted to help me gain an internship placement. At first, I visited with my uncle who lived in

---

41 *Flywheel* is a 2003 American Christian drama film about the unexpected pitfalls that a used car dealer can expect to experience if he suddenly goes honest. Directed and produced by Alex Kendrick.

my city. Aunt Nwamaka was his younger sister. The family welcomed and treated me well. I visited a couple of times and every now and then she would take me to people who she knew in the oil and gas industry to see who could help me get an internship placement. I also visited several companies on my own, both major producers and service oil and gas companies.

For the most part, I thought I was guaranteed a place at one German oilfield servicing firm, Geoservices Nigeria Limited. This happened to be a company where I had an insider connection of someone in a managerial position. Whenever I mentioned his name at the gate, I was guaranteed access into the company. Some days I sat at the visiting room for hours before I got an opportunity to meet with him for a few minutes, but I did not care. I was the one that needed him. He was very nice and always gave me an audience whenever I visited to check for updates about my internship placement with his company. He would assure me that he was making progress and tell me when to check back again. I always did, but nothing really materialized.

My aunt knew him, maybe from church or he may have been a relative. I really do not remember the details or the connection, but going by how I was received and treated, it was a close or very respected connection. I was so sure that I would get in, get a place, and complete my six-month internship with Geoservices. What I did not know was that God had a different plan, a better plan for me. I remember what my aunt always said whenever I came back to her store after my day's journey of toiling in the city to submit applications for an internship position. *"Be prayerful and believe that God will make a way. He always does."* My aunt, just like most members of my extended family, is a good Christian. She attended Seventh Day Adventist services with her family, and I went with them to church every now and then. I also attended my own church on Sundays, so the family knew me as a Christian.

Something happened during the time I was staying at her place though. While still waiting for my internship placement, I went with her to her shop every morning because it was close to the offices where I needed to visit and check on my applications. To beat city traffic, I had to wake up very early (sometimes 4:00 a.m.), help with washing my aunt's car, and get ready for the day's business. Totalfinaelf (now Total) was one oil and gas company that I had my eyes on. I visited them a couple of times; my aunt gave me someone's number to call when I got there. I do not recall what happened, but every time I called or visited the company, he was either away on vacation or was offshore for operations. I continued visiting. I would wait at the gate and call over and over again to no avail. I knew the list for the aptitude test was to come out the following week, so I called and told the secretary about my visit so she could relay my message. At least I had played my part; all I was seeking was an opportunity to take the aptitude test that was required for internship placement at Totalfinaelf. Someone needed to nominate me or get my name added to the list.

I do not blame the companies; a lot of people were applying, and they cannot really accept every application, as there is no easy way to prove student credentials in Nigeria. The technology was not yet in place to identify or weed out fraudulent identities. The very last day before the list was to come out, I was at Totalfinaelf's office very early in the morning, and I stayed through lunch and until the closing time of 4:00 p.m. I watched people come out of the gate to buy calling cards, both Nigerians and foreigners. Young and old. Ladies and gents. Some wore suits, some were dressed in social attire, and some wore tires. Most of the ladies wore pant suits or a nice skirt and well ironed white, yellow, or pink shirt.

They all had one thing in common; they appeared smart in their attire. A badge hung off everyone's neck; they used them to access the entrance gate. At first I did not understand why everyone was showing this badge to a rectangular box by the side of the door. Everyone who needed to open the door raised their badge and showed it to "the magic box," heard a beep or a sound of something opening, opened the door, and walked in. I so wanted to be one of them. Some other days a security man would stand at the door to monitor people entering and leaving the premises just to ensure that they all had their badges. It was not possible to cross the gate if you did not have the badge.

As I watched all this unfold, I began asking myself, could this be how heaven would be? If you do not have a badge, you cannot come in. When you are addicted to the Kingdom, you relate events around you to spiritual matters. This was right in front of me. You needed to know someone in the company to get a visitors badge to cross the gate or to get shortlisted to take the exam. Other companies do the same, which explained why I never got invited for engineering internship placement exams even though I was the best student in my class. I needed to know someone in-house to get a chance. That is when I realized the importance of networking—knowing other professionals in the industry. Schlumberger Oilfield services did visit my school to recruit interns, but I did not do well enough to get their placement. That was my only clear chance. Thank God we have Jesus in heaven. I had a number to dial to enter heaven. I assured myself as I have done all through my life that whatever it will take to get into heaven, I would do.

I do not want to get to the gate only to get turned back. A little digression there, I was telling a story about the day Totalfinaelf released their shortlisted candidates for the internship aptitude test. Of course, I was among the first students to arrive at Totalfinaelf that fateful day. I waited; so many other students waited too. People made calls to the staff they knew who worked in the company. Again, my only contact, Mr. Chidi, who I never got to meet, was still out of the office. It was as if my fate was sealed. My name was not going to be on the list. I remained optimistic. I kept praying and believing God for a breakthrough, maybe a miracle, because at that point that was the only way to describe a positive outcome.

Guess what? The list came out, and everyone rushed to go see the list. I did too, but as I rightly envisaged, my name was not on the list. Well, I had done my part. I was ready to go home. I had not given up though. I told myself that I would be here on Saturday for the company's internship placement exam. Somehow I just believed that God would make a way, and I would be allowed to take the exam. What I did not know was that a lot of students from all over the country had the same plan. When I showed up to write the exam on that day, I saw a crowd, but then only those that had their name on the list were allowed to go through the gate. My plan would not have worked. But God had a better plan for me.

While I was at Totalfinaelf trying all I could to get placement for the aptitude test, my aunt had a discussion with one of her customers about me. She knew I had been going to Totalfinaelf daily and trying to get shortlisted for the internship aptitude test. The lady was so nice and kind and graciously agreed to speak with her husband on my behalf. Her husband was a manager in Totalfinaelf, and later that day we got a call that I should come to their house before 7:00 a.m. on the day of the aptitude test and the husband, a well-respected manager in Totalfinaelf, was to drive his relative and me to the office to sit for the aptitude test. On hearing the news, I was so elated I did not know what to say or do. I could only thank God. You see, miracles do happen. God used my aunt and Mrs. Duze's family to be a blessing to my life. I took the test, passed, and completed my internship with the company. I was made to promise that I would be of good behavior all through my stay at the company.

My aunt vouched for me. She knew my family background, so she had no holdbacks. I also promised to be on my best behavior. It was my first bite of the oil and gas professional experience. I loved it. I wanted more. I wanted to work towards getting another bite. The experience motivated me to even do better when I got back to school, knowing full well that a great future awaited.

Doing Better Than Your Best

Although I was from a family that did not have adequate money at the time, it never crossed my mind to steal a penny from my aunt, but something happened during my stay in Port Harcourt. At times I went to the bank to deposit cash in the millions for my aunt. I would have extra to cover for the bundles that were not complete as they count the bundles with the machine. Whatever change I had left, I always brought back to my aunt. I did not see that as my money. My belief is that I should earn my money. Stealing or swindling has never been my way of life. It is not something I do and not something we do in my family. If something is missing in our house, we usually know that it is either misplaced or we had a strange visitor. We just did not steal; we were not brought up that way. You do not spend another person's money as if it belongs to you. But it so happened one day that after we drove to my aunt's construction site that she approached me and asked if I had any cash with me; I said no. I only had about 50 naira on me; that is less than one dollar.

"*Search yourself; check your back pocket. Do you have another pocket inside your pants?*" my aunt questioned me. At first I was taken aback—why all these questions? Before I knew it, she came towards me to touch my pockets. I was being searched, as if I was lying about the amount of money I had in my pockets. She mentioned that she needed cash to buy gasoline for her car. I told her I was telling the truth and emptied my front and back pockets. I was perplexed, not knowing what was going on. It was later when I got a report that money had been missing at the shop that I was able to put it all together. Money had been missing daily at the shop, and everyone was a suspect, including me. They had not been able to close their accounts without missing a few hundred every now and then. And coming from a family that needed money, I was seen as a possible culprit for the missing money. On normal occasions, I used to help with counting money at close of business. After that experience, I stopped; the environment was not normal anymore. I stayed away from any place they kept their money.

My aunt later found out which of her workers was stealing her money and dismissed him, but she never came to me to apologize, and I never raised the issue with her. Maybe she did not even know that I knew what happened that day. I never mentioned it to anyone, not even my mother. I knew that if I told my mother, she might not allow me to visit my aunt's house again. My mother is like that. She hates for her or any of her kids to be disrespected. She would always fight for us and fight on our behalf. While my aunt was busy trying to figure out if I was stealing her money, one thing she never realized or did not know was that I grew up hearing *"If you are faithful over that which is another's, God will give you your own."* I have heard this over and over again so much that it got stuck in my head. I cannot live otherwise.

As I stated earlier, one person who helped instill this message was Mrs. Ndudi, the director of a private school in Nigeria. She never failed to mention this part of Scripture and what it has meant in her life. It was her motto. I never allowed being poor to affect how I dealt with financial resources that came my way. Count me out when it comes to misappropriating funds. If I have not earned it, I am not spending it. This was the case when I served as the treasurer of the society of petroleum engineers in my alma mater and again when I served as the project leader for four industrial studies group projects as a junior in college. Both positions required me to collect and manage significant amounts of financial resources. On both occasions, my financial report at the end of my tenure received accolades from supervisory authorities, co-leaders, and other team members.

During my final year at FUTO, Dr. Godwin, a professor on sabbatical leave from the University of Alaska, taught us during the harmattan semester. The course was "Reservoir Engineering," and at the end of the semester, I had my first open book exam. He allowed us to come into the exam hall with all our study materials, notebooks, text books, etc. It was a good experience. I liked it. It prevented me from having to cram or memorize the formulas presented in the study manual into my almost filled up brain cells. I made an "A" in his class, and several other students did well in the class too. I was selected to apply to the University of Alaska, and Dr. Godwin promised to help us get funding with the university. I was elated. I took my GRE and TOEFL exams and passed. As God would have it, our degree results were approved shortly after our exams. We defended our thesis in January 2004, and a few months later our results were ready for senate approval. This was in line with the planned convocation ceremony for April 2004.

Everything was working in my favor. I had my transcript sent to the University of Alaska Fairbanks. My graduate study application was successful, and I was offered admission in the program for an MS degree in petroleum engineering. I was also awarded a teaching assistant position that paid all my fees and awarded me a monthly stipend of more than $1,000 per month. Basically, I was being paid to go to school. That was how I viewed it. I liked the idea even though I did not understand all that it entailed. I prayed to God and sought His guidance on the way forward. When I was going through recruitment interviews with different oil companies, I made the furthest headway with Total E & P, an oil and gas company at which I had previously completed a six-month engineering internship. The admission came. I received my immigration documents, made a USA student (F-1) visa application, and scheduled a visa interview appointment for December 6, 2004.

I cannot really tell how I prepared for the interview. I just believed in my qualifications for the program. You see, if I was not eligible, they would not have offered the place to me. That was my mindset. I prayed about the interview. I prayed I would not be asked any question that I could not answer well. In my prayer, I asked for the visa officer to have made up his or her mind in my favor prior to my interview session. At the interview, he only had a few questions for me. Where are you going to? How did you hear about Alaska? What do petroleum engineers do? How will you be funding your program? I expected more questions; instead, he told me to go and return in three days to pick up my passport and visa. I thanked him and left. It was just what I prayed for. On my way out of the consulate, I repeatedly thanked God for His faithfulness. By watching the face of each candidate as they walked out of the consulate, the security officers could tell who was successful in their American visa interviews.

They congratulated me. I was all smiles and joyful. I returned a few days later and got my passport back with a two-year non-immigrant visa stamped on it. Now I had the visa, a document most people in Nigeria would do anything to get, but I still faced challenges, including the challenge of raising about $2,000 for my one-way flight ticket to the "promised land." I thought of how I could raise this money, and many people I hoped would fund me easily turned me down. I do not know why I was surprised. I looked up to men, and they failed me. I began to wonder and ask myself questions, like do I really need to make this journey? I should be comfortable working here in Nigeria as an oil and gas industry employee. I already have a feel of how they are treated in the society.

My older brother Chiemela was kind enough to provide about $1,000 for my journey. I still needed $1,000. I was looking for help, and I ran out of options. Not knowing who else to go to, I handed over everything to God through prayers. In my prayer, I confessed to God that I had tried; if He really wanted me to embark on this journey, I needed Him to make it possible in His own way. I had tried to do it my way and failed.

As the Christmas festive period in 2004 approached, I decided to visit Dr. Godwin and his family at their village home in Imo State. They visit home regularly, and this Christmas season was no exception. I had visited on my own last December. This time, I already had admission and obtained visa to the USA, so I went with my mum. She wanted to thank him and his precious wife also for allowing God to use them to open an avenue for me to relocate to the USA. During our visit, we were received graciously. Both Dr. Godwin and mummy Felicia, as I call her, knew my story, so they looked forward to meeting my mum. They told her how proud they were of her dedication to sending all her children to college, including my humble self.

I was shy, but I understood them, both the things they said and the things they did not say. They are a very loving couple and so kind that one could hardly find any fault in them. As we continued the discussion about my impending trip to the USA, they inquired if I had purchased my ticket; they wanted to know my travel date. To their surprise, I confessed that I had not even raised enough money to pay for my flight ticket. Being a generous family, they offered to provide the remaining part of my travel ticket fund. I was amazed. Mother was so grateful. Mother thanked Dr. Godwin and mummy Felicia, his caring wife; she prayed that God would bless and replenish them. Speechless, with head bowed, I gave God thanks. I thanked God for answered prayers. When I finally raised my head up, I thanked my sponsors and promised to be of good behavior throughout my stay in the United States. They went ahead to give me advice about American life and what to expect when I got to Alaska. I listened carefully to all their advice. Who would not?

I was excited but not ecstatic. It was becoming certain that I was about to be separated from my family when I relocated to an unknown nation. I was not so sure I was ready. Who do I know over there? Are the people friendly, or will they be hostile to me? Will I still be able to go to church? Can I stand the cold? As these questions went over and over through my mind, the knowledge that America was everyone's dreamland helped assuage this fear. Some pastors have even called it the "promised land." Could this be my promised land? I began to pray again. I believed in the word of God that wherever the soles of my feet shall tread upon, I shall possess.[42] So I had no doubt that I would succeed in Alaska. I would be successful in America. I

---

42 Joshua 1:3

continually professed this to myself to assuage or dissuade any form of doubts or fear. Dr. Godwin asked me to stay overnight and said he would give me the money the next day.

Mother had to travel back to Aba alone that night. She was okay with that because she knew I was in good hands. I spent quite some time with Dr. Godwin's family members that day. We watched TV and narrated stories, and when the time came for dinner, we ate. After dinner, I was ushered into a room that had its own separate bathroom. That was how the lovely home was built; every bedroom had its own restroom and bathtub. No room shared bathrooms with another—something I have now gotten accustomed to living in the United States. I did not plan to spend the night, so I did not have any pajamas. The family realized this and was caring enough to present me with pajamas, a really good pair. I do not think it was a guest robe. It was very comfortable. It must have been Dr. Godwin's. When I changed into the pajamas, I put my hand into the side pockets, and lo and behold, there was some good money in it—a bunch of 500 Naira notes. It may have been up to 5,000 naira in total. When I saw the money, it did not even cross my mind to keep it. There was no room to allow the enemy to put any kind of thought in my mind.

Looking back now, I could hear a voice tell me to keep the money; they did not really need it. They are millionaires; 5,000 naira is no big deal to them. I ignored that voice. I did not even consider such temptation in my heart. I was a born again Christian. I believed in earning my income; if I have not worked for it and the owner did not give it to me, I am not taking what does not belong to me. I was a man of integrity, and I was not about to sell my birth right for a morsel of yam porridge. I took the money back to Nkem, Dr. Godwin's niece who brought the pajamas to me. "I saw this money in the pocket of the pajamas you gave to me; it must belong to Dr. Godwin. Please could you return it to him? Thank you," I said as she opened their bedroom door to answer to my knock. She appeared surprised, took the money, and told me goodnight.

As I walked back to my room that night, I was happy knowing that I had done the right thing. I slept peacefully. Looking back, I feel that I passed a character test that night. It did not occur to me at the time of the event, but looking back, I believe it was a test of my character and integrity. I could have kept the money, but then I could lose the $1,000 they planned on giving to me in the morning. Or if they gave me the money, they would easily make a decision to deal with me carefully. But passing that test made them accept me as one of them, a member of their family, and they welcomed me and were eager and ready to help me whenever I needed help. They remain one of my greatest allies. And I remain grateful to God, who brought them into my life.

Deal Honestly with People

During my mum's visit in the summer of 2010, we went to a hair product shop along Westheimer Road on the west side of Houston, Texas. It was required that one use a hair cover before trying on the various United Nations of hair products available. I say United Nations because they had Brazilian hair, Indian hair, all kinds of human hair. We collected one head cover, sold for about a dollar, without paying for it. The plan was to pay during our purchase of whichever product my mother chose. It so happened that after my mum made her choice for a couple of the products that she liked, we made payments only for the hair products and forgot to add the head cover as part of the bill. Fortunately, we remembered when we got to the car, and the following conversation ensued.

> "*Ah Mum, did we pay for the stuff you used to cover your head before trying on the wigs?*" I asked.
>
> "*I don't think so; do we need to pay for that?*" Mother asked.
>
> "*Yes, the cashier asked that we pay when we are checking out,*" I replied. "*Let me go back and see the cashie*r."

Mother agreed with me, and that was exactly what I did; I went back and informed the cashier of the mistake. It was just a dollar, but I wanted a clear conscience. The cashier looked amazed. After he recovered from his surprise, he looked at me and thanked me for my honesty. He confessed to me that many would have just driven away but that what I did made him believe that there are good people out there. At the shop were four friendly African American ladies who were waiting to pay for some hair products. On hearing my exchange or conversation with the cashier, one of them called out to me on my way out and said something that is still very fresh in my memory. In fact, I can still recall her voice and her facial expression as she called out to me.

"Uncle, you didn't have to be that honest; I would have just driven off," she said. Turning around, I smiled at her, and I cannot recall if I had any response other than the smile. If I did, my response probably would have been that I needed to have a clear conscience. Had it happened today, my response would have been different. It would be an opportunity to proclaim that it was the Jesus in me. It was an opportunity to let the world see the Jesus in me.

On another occasion, while unpacking the goods I got from Walmart, I realized that I had a gallon of milk included in my groceries that I did not plan to purchase nor did I pay for. After carefully reviewing my receipt and verifying that there was no charge for milk, I knew I had a decision to make. Return the milk or keep it. Thoughts started flying through my head. This is Walmart, and it is a perishable good, so is it returnable? Will they accept it? What will they do for a returned milk? Do I need the product? I thought of driving to the shop to pay for the product. I decided against buying the product because I would not be able to finish it before it reached its expiration date, which was about 10 to 14 days. So I made a decision to return the product. Several questions raced through my mind. How much is this gallon of milk? How about your time? You know time is money? You do not have any other business at Walmart;

it is a total waste of your time. And how sure are you they will accept it? As these questions flowed through my mind, I considered not going anymore, but something pricked my spirit again, and by the time I realized where I was, I was speaking to the two customer assistant officers at Walmart.

"*I saw this gallon of milk in my grocery bag; I didn't plan to buy one, and I'm sure I didn't pay for one either. Someone else might have paid for it and forgot to pick it up, so I'm returning it,*" I said.

"Okay…" the attendant responded while collecting the gallon of milk from me with a surprised look on her face.

I do not know if it was my accent that she had issues with or if it was the fact that they were not used to seeing people return products that they did not pay for. They thanked me for my honesty and promised to look out for the customer who had paid for the product if he or she ever came back. I do not know what I learned from this experience, but I want to believe that God might have used the opportunity to minister to those two ladies that honesty is still the best policy. And you know what? I could visualize the two ladies getting home that day and telling a story of this African American young man who returned a product that he did not pay for that he saw in his grocery bag.

I thought of them having a discussion about it. I see them seeking answers to "what would you have done?" Do you think he did the right thing and why? You, the reader of this book, do you think I did the right thing? You see, it is not always about us. If only we can see the big picture, we will always, always deal honestly with people. God surely could have used this to minister to someone's life, and it is my prayer that through your honest living, God will bring men and women to right standing with Him. Treat others the way you would like to be treated.

I recall my experience on September 16, 2012. I went to an African store to purchase some African food products. After I left the shop, before I could drive off, the cashier of the store rushed out and called to inform me that she had double charged me for one of the products. She apologized and asked that I shop for more products equivalent to the extra charge. She could not give me a cash refund because I had paid with a credit card, and the difference was not big enough to warrant the fees involved in credit card purchases or refunds. I was so grateful for her honesty.

My mind definitely ran back to times in my life that I had done the same thing. I told myself, "*Oh how honest a lady; not everyone would do that.*" I appreciated her honesty, and I like going back there for my African food shopping. I scanned through the shop and decided to purchase ripe plantains, which came in handy that weekend as I fried some of them with yam and ate it with a delicious fish stew for dinner. It was such a quick meal that I had to think back on how I even got the plantains in the first place. Since then I have visited the store whenever I need. Like they say, what goes around comes around. And you, too, can get paid with your own coins. Keep in mind too, as Og Mandino once said, "Always do your best. What you plant now, you will harvest later."[43]

Commit to Other People's Advancement

When it comes to academics, I like the inspiring story of one of my mentors, Dr. Ben Carson, a renowned retired American neurosurgeon. Among other surgical innovations, Carson did pioneering work on the successful separation of conjoined twins joined at the head. His early life was comprised of everything that could possibly preclude success. And yet at an early age, his mother taught him not to make any excuses for his failures; she never accepted any excuse that he tried to offer. It was one of the important things that his mother taught him. You know, if you keep rejecting excuses, people will get used to it and start seeking solutions.

His mother read the assignments he turned in to her and put check marks everywhere on the pages. What Ben Carson and his

---

[43] Mandino, Og. The Greatest Salesman in the World. Bantam (January 5, 2011)

brother did not know, though, was that their mother could not read. Ben Carson's mom was committed to his advancement. After a while, Ben Carson began to enjoy reading. He read about prominent men and connected the dots; he found out that how successful one gets depends only on him. He hated poverty with a passion, but he stopped hating poverty after he realized it was just a passing phase in his life. He was determined to turn out successful. Today, Ben Carson has a foundation that looks out for intellectual stars.

In his book *America the Beautiful*,[44] he asks repeatedly, what does the intellectual star win? The best mathematics student or the most outstanding scientist or science student? What do they win? Who invites them to award dinners or recognizes them as intellectual giants? Today, we worship athletes—point guards, quarterbacks, sports captains, and you name it—and forget the intellectual stars. He asserted, and rightfully so, that it is not helping America or the world in general. He established the Carson Foundation to give scholarships to smart students. Schools get trophies. Smart students get invited to luncheons where they are treated like superstars. It puts things in the right perspective. The Carson Foundation's goal in establishing libraries in schools is to prevent students from joining the 30% of high school dropouts or 40% of four year college dropouts in the United States. The Carson Foundation scholars are required to spend a set amount of hours in the library each term.

As a student and continuing post-graduation, in 2005/2006 I instituted an awards program for the best student as measured per GPA for each level—male and female—and an award for the best overall graduating student (final year) for Winners Campus Fellowship at my alma mater. This has been in place since I graduated from FUTO. I knew that receiving awards as the best student, in my freshman year, motivated me to strive to stay on top, and my intent by the grace of God was to create that same feeling in others.

---

44 Carson, Ben. America the Beautiful: Rediscovering What Made This Nation Great. Zondervan (January 24, 2012)

It is easier to get to the top than it is to remain there. It is my prayer that we will continue this trend and hopefully someday establish a scholarship foundation that could aid smart students in achieving their dreams of education. God is no respecter of persons; if you do what opens heavens, God will bless you. In summer 2009, I chose to remain in school and complete my dissertation so I could begin fulltime employment in October of that year.

What it entailed was about three to four months of living in the United States and fending for myself without any income. This happened because my supervisor research program did not sponsor students during the summer. I had to pay my school fees for the classes I registered for that summer. I had to pay my monthly house rent, feed myself, fuel my car, and every other routine upkeep cost that one could think of. I knew about all of this prior to making the decision to not go for a summer internship. It was one of the hardest decisions I have had to make in my career.

Three months later, the result of spending without any source of income was an empty account. At the same time, I got a call that it was time again for the annual award that I instituted in my alma mater back in Nigeria. I did not know what to do. I did not have enough resources to do this for the year. I was tempted to cancel it for the year. The temptation to cancel was strong. I had already tried earlier to borrow $1,000 from a friend who had already started work in the oil and gas industry but without success. As I thought about it, and as the day of the event approached, I knew that I was not going to cancel the award. It would not be fair for the people who had worked to be in a position to win the awards. But to provide for the awards, I was required to empty both my checking and savings account of the funds, and that was what I did. I emptied my bank account, and then a miracle happened.

On my way to send the money to my campus fellowship's president, who I had been in touch with, I made a call to get details on whose name I should use to send the money for the award. During the call,

Doing Better Than Your Best

I was informed that schools had been closed down for a while and the graduation ceremony was going to be on hold until ASUU ended their strike. I was shocked; God had made a way for me. The story reminds me of Abraham's willingness to sacrifice his only son, Isaac.[45] I was about to sacrifice my Isaac, all of my bank account funds that could be withdrawn. And I found out that our God, who sees in secret and who knows the intentions of our hearts, made a way for me. That bought me some time.

As I thought about everything that day, I felt happy, like someone who had just passed a major life test. There and then I knew that I needed to maintain the mind-set that I am blessed to be a blessing. I knew that God had not forgotten me and that He was about to do something new in my life. As I mentioned earlier, this led to a very insightful period in my life. I discovered the answer to the challenges I faced with my dissertation, which meant I was ready to graduate.

Everything began to make sense again. I danced and praised God. This was a period when I was still struggling with making headway in my dissertation research. I had tons of data, but I just did not know what to do with it. Did I need a different kind of data for my analysis? Did I need to build a different grid system? Did I need to look at the available data in a different light? All these questions troubled my mind each day. Three months had already passed, and things were not looking so rosy. But that same week, I woke up in the middle of the night, and an insight came to me. It was so clear that I can still remember it. Do this, do that, analyze this data this way, combine the data in this format, you will have a trend, and you will find explanations for the behavior that you are looking for. Eureka! That was it! My dissertation was done, and I was ready to graduate. Well, it was not quite that easy. It took another two months of computer simulation work and data analysis to prove the theory and present my data to my supervisor.

---

45 Genesis 22

Chapter 

Do Right

"Do the do's and you won't have to worry about doing the don'ts." ~ Dr Creflo Dollar

Events in life have taught me that the best way to escape evil is to pursue good. Having set values and standards that you live with helps to guide your actions. In his book, *Dare to Be*,[46] John Mason stated and I quote, "To know what is right and not do it is as bad as doing wrong." The first time I read this statement, I brought out my notebook and made a note of it. In my youth, I served and worshiped God whenever the opportunity called. Going to church was more than a routine; it was a way of life for me. I looked forward to it. It was my greatest source of joy. In a way, I was feeding my spirit, which was guiding me towards doing right. I had a living conscience. I kept

---

[46] Mason, John. *Dare to Be: 70 Questions That Lead to Life's Most Important Answers.* Bridge-Logos Publishers. 2006

my head and heart going in the right direction, and I did not have to worry about my feet. I like how Dr. Creflo Dollar[47] puts it: "Do the do's and you won't have to worry about doing the don'ts."

When I say no, it is not because I want to be different or I want to make a name for myself. It is to remain in the centre of God's will for my life. What is your motive for saying no or saying yes and for doing what it is you do? As long as we are on this earth, there will be people who will go out of their way to do us wrong, and it behooves us to not pay them back in their own coin. By His grace, I always try to be the better person and not pay wrong for wrong. Know this truth: We pay the price for our future by how we live our life today. My advice to anyone reading this book is to do the right thing even when nobody is watching you. When others are goofing off, stay the course and do the right thing. God is keeping the records, so keep sowing seeds of a disciplined life. Treat even people who do not deserve it well. Do not get weary of doing good things, and in due season, you will reap your reward. I always believe that my promotion is around the corner. My breakthrough is around the corner. So when people treat me poorly, I do not let them get under my skin. The saying goes that you cannot stop a bird from flying over your head, but you surely can prevent it from perching on your head.

I believe that it is the testimonies that people give about me when I am not around that count, not the ones they give in my presence. So I try my best to be consistent in the way I live my life, ensuring that my words match my actions. It is testimonies when you are absent that will bring you breakthroughs and open doors. They are avenues of favor, so cultivate them. Think of how you feel when you get a good report about someone from unknown sources that you run into; it is a good feeling. How about creating such feelings in people when they hear about you? It takes a commitment to do the right thing, no matter what, to have such a life.

---

47   Creflo Augustus Dollar, Jr. is a televangelist, a pastor, and the founder of the non-denominational World Changers Church International based in Fulton County, Georgia.

To maintain your joy, let the joy of the Lord be your strength. God has the power to change times and seasons. It does not matter what the time has been for you. The good news is that God can turn your situation around. No matter how heavy the night is, it does not stop the morning from coming. No matter how heavy the sorrow, it does not stop joy from coming once God has decided that your time has come. When I think of what anger could do to someone, I recall my sister's response when someone offended her.

She was so angry that she boldly stated that she was going to use a knife to kill my brother (the offender) at night while he slept. She was warning him to make sure he stayed awake because if he did not, that day would be the last day that he would see in his life. As a boy, I watched in total bewilderment as these words angrily flowed out of my sister's lips. As I reviewed her statements, I began to ask myself questions: Is it really worth it to offend people? What if she goes ahead to fulfill her threats? Can people really say these things when they are angry? I guess these questions came naturally to me because I was someone who believed that my words mattered, so if I am going to say something, I want to make it count. I try to make promises that I can keep. I try to make my words my bond. They matter to me. People say I do not say much, and that explains why. I like to think of the implications of what I say before I utter a word. While this might not be the best approach to life and living, I will confess that it has helped me to stay out of trouble.

So I began to wonder about what I should say when I am offended. What could be the best way not to say these mean things to people? How about not saying anything when you are angry but waiting until you cool off and are able to speak reasonably with the person who offended you? People might see you as a weakling, but you will be maintaining a very good virtue. That has been my motto. When you stay in peace, God will not only fight your battles but He will pay you double for your troubles. It pays to stay calm and collected. Do not let your circumstances control you. Mad people like to make other people mad; do not let them. Do not play religion; be a Christian. Do not be great at preaching but not practicing. Be consistent in your actions. Stay away from anger. It hurts only you. I see it this way: If I am right, then there is no need for me to get angry, and if I am wrong, then I also do not have any right to get angry. Every test in our life makes us bitter or better; every problem can make us or break us. The choice is ours whether we become victims or victorious. Like I said earlier, when you stay in peace, God will not only fight for your battles but He will pay you double for your trouble.

Sometime in 2012 I was involved in a conflict during a soccer incident. A player from the opposing team, who I will call Willy, felt that I wronged him in the way I attacked him to strip the ball from him. Willy went bananas and called me all kind of names, names I do not feel comfortable mentioning here. They were curse words, very offensive to me as I am not use to being called such names. It hurt. It was a painful experience hearing him say all that. Everyone that was in the field was shocked by his response to my tackle. I stopped and looked back at Willy, and everyone did the same. Then other players encouraged me to play on; that they did not see any infringement that called for a foul play. So we continued the game.

Writing this story reminded me of a time when I was mad at someone and acted out of character, calling a young lady that I cared about words that are not graceful. It pained my heart that I acted out of character, and though it has been more than four years since the incident and we have reconciled, I picked up my phone and called her; I apologized once again and confessed that I really acted out of character. She was shocked and appreciated the call. I told her how someone used similar words on me recently; it made me understand how she felt, and I felt so sorry for what I might have put her through. It was a restoring moment for me.

Now back to the soccer event. Another opportunity came where both of us had to go for a loose ball. Again I shielded him from the ball, and obviously still angered from the prior incident, he threw a punch at me. His plan was to hit me on the face, but he got me right behind my right ear. Ouch! Did you make that sound? I bet you did. I could hear you ask, how did that make you feel? What did you do next? I plan to tell you, I just wanted you to think of what your response could have been if you were in my shoes. Would you have returned a punch? He is a smaller guy, so I am very sure that I could have taken him down or at least put up a fight. Maybe I could have shown him a bit of my tae kwon do skill; you know, the skills I have learnt over the years watching Jackie Chan and Chris Tucker in *Rush Hour 1, 2 & 3*.[48]

But no! I chose to be a better person and not pay wrong for wrong. I realized that he had allowed his anger to get the better of him, and I chose not to do the same. You know what my first instinct was, but I had already chosen not to lose my joy for any cause. I chose to do what I am asking you to do. No matter how offended you are, stay calm and collected. This was not an easy decision to make on the spur of the moment. It was a decision I ought to have made before leaving home for work that day, prior to the incident. I just picked up the soccer ball, looked at him, and walked off the field. People rushed to hold both of us away from each other. Behind me I could see people holding him back, telling him not to do anything crazy other than what he had already done. I do not know what would have happened if I had made a different decision that day. May be we would have been arrested and spent a night in jail, or worse still, one of us could have been hospitalized. This was another experience with anger that taught me the importance of not offending people and staying calm and collected at all times.

People wonder why they are not happy. I like the illustration Pastor Joel Osteen gave at a Sunday service in Lakewood Church: It is because they keep giving away joy when things do not go their way.

---

48 *Rush Hour 1, 2 & 3* are martial arts buddy action comedy films. The *Rush Hour* series stars Jackie Chan and Chris Tucker who respectively reprise their roles as Inspector Lee and Detective Carter.

They give away joy when they cannot find their car key. They give away joy when they get to the laundry and their clothes are not ready. It encouraged me to take inventory of my life and find out what I am losing my joy for. I chose to always strive to not give up my joy over small things. Is it really worth it to lose your joy over the fact that you cannot find a parking spot? It is not really that big of a deal to be five minutes late to a soccer game.

Chapter 12

The Gift of Life

Life is a free gift from God. It is not something that we earn nor is it something that must be paid back. Realizing this, I gracefully accept each day I am alive with gratitude. I never asked to be born. No one gave me the opportunity to choose my parents. I get to pick my friends, but I do not get to pick my family. I had no choice over my genes or blood type. I did not select my siblings. I never requested for Dr. Godwin to be my hero and allow God to use him to provide an opportunity for me to relocate to the United States of America. I was not given the opportunity to approve or disapprove of the man who would be my father and the woman who would be my mother. And the times into which I was born were not of my making or my choosing. In fact, my parents were not expecting me or planning to have another child just yet when I showed up. I was that child that people never wanted my mum to keep.

They were not happy that my mum, who had just given birth the year before, was pregnant again. With my dad being away in graduate school, they gave my mum a tough time. They called her names. Not knowing that she was pregnant did not help matters; hence my first name—"Chinenye-nwa," meaning "it is God who gives a child." As my being here today shows, my parents chose to keep me. They chose that name because they believed that my conception was an act of God, not just because they made love. My dad was in graduate school then, studying for his master's degree in Religious Studies at the great University of Jos, about 800 kilometers from Amachi Nsulu, my home town, where my mother resided with my other siblings. I was well fed, having stayed in my mum's womb for almost 10 months.

I was born in the humblest of places—a maternity home—with the services of an experienced midwife. It is just one of those things that happen when you live in the village, a rural community. Thank God I made it. Thank God I am still here today. I do not take being alive lightly. Life is a gift, and I am committed to living and cherishing every moment that there is. Such a mind-set helps me relate with people with ease and stay away from offending them. Today, I am looked up to by many as one of the brightest young men in my extended family, but while my mother was pregnant with me, the same people asked her not to keep me. They talked about family planning, of having two or three years between your kids. I am glad my parents made the wise decision to keep me. You never can tell; the child you choose to keep could potentially be the life saver of your family.

I was made to understand at an early age that God's plan is better for my life. Like Daniel and the Hebrew boys in my book of Bible stories, it was inculcated in my heart that if I did not bow to the graven image, I would not burn. From the Bible story of Joseph,[49] I learnt that if I did not fall into the trap of fornication or adultery, that

---

49 Genesis 39

God's plan, which is better for my life, would ensue. I had a vision of a glorious future that like Joseph, I refused to allow Satan take away from me.

As a boy, I played with my peers when I got the opportunity, did my homework, and sought opportunities to grow by learning something new every day. Abraham Lincoln stated that he did not think much of a man who is not wiser today than he was yesterday. That was one of my major life philosophies: to learn something new each day! It could be a new word, a scientific term, a Bible character, life stories gleaned from a book, or someone's life story translated in words. The books I read in elementary school, along with mother's advice on the importance of education, made me believe and understand the importance of delayed gratification.

The precepts of the writers of the books I read as well as my mother's advice called for me to keep my hands clean, to take responsibilities for my actions, and to do what is required of me. These were among the many godly characteristics that I desired to achieve. And know that keeping your hands clean, here, refers to doing what is right. As Bishop T. D. Jakes[50] once said: *"You will never see any genuine success without evidence of delayed gratification."* For me, delayed gratification was easy because as I stated earlier, I was so busy or lost doing the do's that I didn't have the time to worry about not doing the don'ts. Discipline and honesty were my watch words. I lived by them. I learned something new each day. After all, by the words of the legendary basketball coach, John Wooden, "It is what you learn after you know it all that counts."

Hence, I made a decision, before I understood all the challenges I would have to face along the way, to get to my desired career and become a petroleum engineer. Later, I discovered all that I needed to achieve this and reach my desired goal of a good life, something

---

50 Bishop T. D. Jakes is a charismatic leader, visionary, provocative thinker, and entrepreneur who serves as senior pastor of The Potter's House, a global humanitarian organization and 30,000-member non-denominational American church located in Dallas.

better than what I was going through, something better than the life my parents offered. I realized that to achieve this goal—my career as a petroleum engineer—I had to create this world by achieving academic excellence that would open the doors to that career. I held on to that hope that if I did what is required, made good grades, and had a good character, God would bless the works of my hand and cause me to fulfill my goals and achieve my life visions. To get there, I would be required to finish not only secondary school and five years of college, but I would also have to do well in school. It was a choice that had to be made in the beginning—a choice already made for me if I am to get there.

With Mum being a teacher, I never really attended nursery school or kindergarten. I just followed Mum to school always. When I was four, Mum made me stay in the elementary one class and came to pick me up after school. I made good grades and was among the best in the class, but since I was not registered, I could not go with the other kids to elementary two. The next school year, I had to repeat elementary one. One other student and I were always competing for first position while I attended Umuobasi Amavo Community Primary School from my primary one to primary four. To my advantage, I did very well.

Then, after my dad's untimely departure from the earth, we moved into the city, and I was enrolled into a new school where Mum taught. Again, I loved school and learning. Some teachers liked me; some did not. The ones who did not like me complained that my writing was so bad, and I still ended up being among the top three students in their class. They kept prodding me to improve my writing; one day, my teacher called four other teachers and was showing them my notes. Her complaint was how could someone with such bad writing be one of the best students in her class. That is what happens when your head runs faster than your hand can put thoughts in writing. It was a show of mixed feeling. I was a child, and I did not know what to say or how to respond. I never brought this up at home. I knew if I had told Mum, she would tell my teacher to stop worrying about my writing. My mum knew that I just wrote so fast that I did not really care about how it looked. And she knew that my writing might have been bad, but more often than not, my answers were correct.

Still, I loved doing school work from an early age; it helped me to figure things out. I liked to know why, how, and what and learn new words. I loved science and how it explains things around us. My insatiable curiosity led me to read my textbooks as if they contained the secrets of life. I was basically a nerd—a born again nerd. This was not a good combination to get the girls; I knew that, and I did not care. I came to terms with the fact that life is a product of personal adventure. If you must have good success, then you must, as a matter of fact and truth, accept responsibilities by cultivating a winning attitude. You must carefully and meticulously obey and do your part. No matter how you love someone, no matter how close you are to someone, you cannot eat for the person. I realized that no matter how mother loved me, she could not eat for me. I understood that if I failed, it was my fault; if I succeeded, it was my actions that would allow me to succeed.

At an early age, I made up my mind to accept responsibility for what becomes of me. Looking at people who mattered and who I saw were successful, it was so clear that their achievements were a product of the responsibilities they had accepted in the past. When I see medical professionals, I tell myself that these are people who have paid the price to get there. When I see an engineer, I see someone who has paid his price by taking science courses in high school and four to five years of engineering classes in college to get to where he or she is today. I did not see them as the lucky ones; I saw them as people who had paid the price to get where they are.

Suffice it to say that I believed that where I would be tomorrow would be a product of the responsibilities I took going forward. I was not about to do anything or run away from any responsibility that would take me to the top. I believed in the popular saying that when you run away from the scars, you never get to wear the stars. It is pain that brings you gain. I chose to face life like someone who knows where he is going. I began to see exams as opportunities to get to my next level, and I had no other choice but to prepare extremely well for them and do a good job to ensure that I gave it better than my best effort. I somehow became what people call a perfectionist. A little bit of that is good for you, not too much of it. Like they say, too much of anything is bad.

Growing up, there were so much that I did not have in terms of wants and needs, but I did not allow that to steal my joy. I remained content with what I had and what we had as a family, relying on God's gifts and talents upon my life. Through my days on earth, my life has shown me that life is a series of decisions. One needs to be mindful of what he or she is basing his or her decision on—the Word, friends, parents, world values, public opinions, etc. This book highlights some decisions that I have made in life and how they turned out with the hope that someone can learn from them.

My goal in life has always been to make decisions that will help exploit my gifts to be a blessing to others. I can hear someone say, "But I don't know what my gift is!" So let me help you; your gift is the thing that everyone celebrates about you, though you may take it for granted. I like how Michelle Hammond put it in her book: "The reason is no big deal to you is because it's your natural gift."[51]

Maybe it is inherent to your nature to be creative, detail oriented, good with children, sharp with numbers, given to hospitality, an effective counselor…whatever it is, God wants you to use your God-given abilities to bless others around you. In the process, you will prosper—not just materially but emotionally and spiritually. You will be filled with the satisfaction of knowing that you live a life that matters to God, to others, and even yourself. There is no greater sense of joy and peace than to lay your head down at the end of the day knowing that you were used to help someone or to add something to

---

51   Hammond, Michelle. *Sassy, Single, and Satisfied*. Harvest House Publishers (August 1, 2010)

someone else's life. And if you are getting paid for it, well, that is even better! We are blessed to be a blessing. I believe that God's dream for my life is to bless me abundantly so that I can be a blessing to others.

Attitude

When I started my PhD program at the University of Oklahoma in 2006, I was not so sure I was going to complete it because my friends and school colleagues were getting job offers. I even received one to relocate to Europe. It was a confusing stage in my life. I prayed about it, and while I sought divine guidance, I made a decision that no matter what the future held, I was going to put in my best in all my classes as if I was going to complete the program. I am so glad I did because if I was nonchalant about my coursework and focused on getting a job, I could have a grade that I would possibly regret for the rest of my life. I put in my best into all my courses that semester and I got all "A"s. Then I was ready to take a job, go work for a while, and then come back for my PhD program. I did not make that decision; I got a summer internship with BP America. Hence I stayed to complete my program. I consider myself humble, having learned from church that pride disqualifies and disconnects you from grace and makes you a candidate for disgrace. Today, if I did not inform you or no one else tells you, you will never know that I have a doctorate degree in engineering.

The longer I live, the more I realize the importance of attitude in life. Attitude, to me, is more important than one's past, than education, than money, than circumstances, than failures, than successes, than what other people think or say or do. It is more important than appearance, giftedness, or skill. It will make or break a company, a church, a home, or an individual. The remarkable thing is that we have a choice every day regarding the attitude we will embrace for that day. We cannot change our past; we cannot change the fact that people will act in a certain way. We cannot change the inevitable. The only thing we can do is plan on the one thing we have, and that

Doing Better Than Your Best

is our attitude. I am convinced that life is 10% what happens to me and 90% how I react to it. And so it is with you. Winston Churchill[52] once said, and I agree, "Success is not final, failure is not fatal: it is the courage to continue that counts."

I like to take charge of my attitude. The future belongs to an uncommon man with uncommon attitude. That is the right attitude to have. I focus on the future. I focus on the solution, since I am solution oriented. I always look out for the good—the valuable lesson in my failures. It helps me to continually improve on the behaviors or attitudes of my life. I like to think on paper, taking my time to write out every detail of the problem, and then taking the next logical step to solve it. This helped me when I was preparing for job interviews and when I actually interviewed for a job. To prepare, I wrote the questions down and noted my answers to possible interview questions. I did not cram, but I had a life story I could link to any possible behavioral questions that came my way.

Hear what Andre Previn, a German-American pianist, conductor, and composer, who is considered one of the most versatile musicians in the world with four Academy awards and eleven Grammy awards, said about practice: "If I miss a day of practice, I know it. If I miss two days, my manager knows it. If I miss three days, my audience knows it." I believe in the wise saying that the secret of your future lies in your daily routine. One can easily predict the future of a man by observing what he does every day. I chose to make every day of my life pay a price through study and endeavor for the success that I desire in the future. I would like to end this chapter with one of Martin Luther King Jr.'s famous quotes: "Whatever your life's work is, do it well. A man should do his job so well that the living, the dead, and the unborn could do it no better."

---

52 Sir Winston Leonard Spencer-Churchill, (30 November 1874 – 24 January 1965) was a British politician who was the Prime Minister of the United Kingdom from 1940 to 1945 and again from 1951 to 1955.

Chapter 13

The Higher Life

I recall the first Bible recitation that I did as a boy. It was taken from the Book of Proverbs. It states: "The fear of the LORD is the beginning of knowledge, but fools despise wisdom and instruction. My son, hear the instruction of thy father, and forsake not the law of thy mother, for they shall be an ornament of grace unto thy head, and chains about thy neck. My son, if sinners entice thee, consent thou not.[53]"

I recall another one from the same Book of Proverbs: "Reprove not a scorner, lest he hate thee; rebuke a wise man, and he will love thee. Give instruction to a wise man, and he will be yet wiser; teach a just man, and he will increase in learning. The fear of the LORD is the beginning of wisdom, and the knowledge of the holy is understanding."[54] I learned this as a member at that time of Qua

---

53 Proverbs 1:7-10
54 Proverbs 9:8-10

Iboe Church Abayi International (now United Evangelical Church), named so because the Portuguese missionaries that established the church in Nigeria came in through the Qua Iboe River terminal in Akwa Ibom State, Nigeria.

All the children in our church looked forward to the children's harvest ceremony that occurs every year, myself included. We loved it for several reasons. It is a thanksgiving service, and all the mothers go to church and cook for the whole congregation to eat, so we looked forward to the delicious jellof rice with succulent and well marinated beef or goat meat. Another event at the ceremony is that children take turns to recite different Bible verses either in Igbo or in English, and some who have prepared well enough could recite the same scripture in both languages. The longer your recitation, the more applause you get, and the more people come out to throw money at you as a reward for your efforts. I recall getting a standing ovation on several occasions for my recitations.

Yes, I like to put in my best in everything I do. I am very competitive; that is my drive. If anything is worth doing, I have always strived for the best. To be the best, you have to pay the price. All these experience growing up helped prepared me for the life I had to live in college—a life that required discipline and focus to achieve desired goals. These recitations were another driving force to participate and excel. They were an early learning of reward for learning, as the money that gets thrown at you while you are giving your recitation belongs to you. The children who made the most money were children who either made very long recitations such as going through a long chapter that ministered to people or little kids who could barely utter a line or verse in the Bible, the most popular one being "train up a child in the way he should go and when he is old, he will not depart from it."[55] Some years we could have up to five kids reciting the same scripture with their crying voice…"train up a child in the way he should grooowwww…" and the baby cries

---

55 Proverbs 22:6

through his presentation. Another popular one was "children obey your parents in the Lord, for this is right."[56] As I pen these thoughts, I am reminded of my childhood days. Just recalling those moments makes me want to be a kid again. Those were precious moments.

I understood at an early age that you will never enjoy certain things in life except through the proper use of your communication privilege with heaven. Certain doors in life will never open to you until you properly engage your communication link with God through prayer. As a family, we had a set time to pray in the morning when we rose and at night before we went to bed. We all had opportunities to lead the family in prayer. My parents made us take turns leading the family in praying; even I, at the age of six, was expected to take the lead. I will not say we were all prayer warriors, but it instilled in us the importance of prayer and relying on God to guide us through the day.

We had a timetable, and we all knew that no one goes to bed until Dad is done listening to the evening news and calling everyone to join together in his bedroom, and sometimes in the living room, for family prayers. Usually we would sing a few praise songs and then worship songs; Dad would teach from the Word, and later whoever had the turn to pray would lead the closing prayer. It was not always easy, but it taught me a valuable life lesson as a boy—that prayer every day was, and should be, a part of my life. Father was such a good teacher; as a matter of fact, he was planning to join a pastoral ministry after he retired from teaching.

Understand, too, that we ought to never be too busy to pray, and we should pray without ceasing throughout the day, as the Holy Spirit instructs. I can remember asking my dad, "Why do we pray every day and night? Is the one we prayed in the morning not enough?" And his response was that you can never pray too much. And this is in line with the scripture, which says, "Men ought always to pray, and not faint."[57] That is why the word of God admonishes us to pray always, to "Pray without ceasing."[58]

---

56 Ephesians 6:1
57 Luke 18:1
58 1 Thessalonians 5:17

Every strong relationship thrives on the maintenance of a very good communication link between the parties involved, and prayer is our link with God that serves that purpose. It enhances the strength of our relationship with our heavenly Father. I pray about everything, from the simple request that traffic lights act in my favor or that I get a good parking spot at the mall to asking God to fulfill His promise of helping me through any challenge whatsoever that I may go through. My dad was a scripture union member, a committed one. My parents paid attention to their spiritual life, and as I stated earlier, they were both born again Christians.

So we always went to the annual retreat that is hosted in the city of Aba, a yearly retreat led by Apostle Umar Ukpai. Looking back, I can say that those nights were probably the few nights, maybe the only nights, I spent away from my family home. How important was it that the few nights I spent away from home growing up were nights spent in His presence. No wonder, when I look back today, I find my greatest source of joy occurring when I am dwelling in His presence. Ask me the exact day that I gave my life to Christ and I will not be able to tell you.

But whether through the gathering of the saints at church or listening to men of God on television (thank God for technology!) or just doing random acts that bring glory to the name of the Father and show that I am acknowledging that Christ lives in me, I have fullness of joy. On the other side, I feel horrible when I find myself in compromising situations, things that do not bring glory to His name. A lesson I have learned over the years is to stay with God if I want my joy to be full. One thing I always do is to get up and stand my ground against the devil in prayers to secure my glorious destiny in God. In line with the scripture,[59] "Submit yourselves therefore to God. Resist the devil, and he will flee from you."

Going to church helped build up my faith, making me who I am today. I recall some of the sermons I heard growing up; the one

---

59 James 4:7

on marriage really stuck with me as particularly important. Marry someone who has the fear of God in her heart. The fear of God will not allow someone to sacrifice you for money. It will cause the person to have the right priorities. When people cheat, it is not because they do not love you; it is because they do not have the fear of God in them. Pastor used the story of Joseph to illustrate this point. Think of what Joseph said when Potiphar's wife tried to woo him to bed:[60] "... because thou art his wife: how then can I do this great wickedness, and sin against God?"

Why do we stay away from sin? If it is not because of the fear or love of God, then it is not going to stand the test of time. By the fear of God, I do not mean a worldly reverence of His presence, as in being scared, the way people fear mighty men or cultic men or men with dubious affairs. I mean realizing that there is a God above who loves us so much that He gave his only begotten son that whosoever believeth in Him should not perish but have everlasting life. My desire to have this everlasting life and understand the path that He has set for me is what guarantees the fear of God in my life. I know that there is a reward in obedience and in obeying His words. I understood at a young age that any short pleasure is not worth the sidetrack from my glorious destiny.

When I obey, I believe a blessing is always attached to it. Wonder what you miss when you do not obey. When I exhibit bold obedience, I never know where God is going to lead me. I do not know what doors God will open for me. But I have faith in the saying that not only are His ways higher than our ways, but also His thoughts for me are thoughts of good and not of evil to give me a future with hope. We can all obey when it is easy and when things are going well. What about when it is not ordinary? How about when God wants you to do more than going to church and paying your tithe? When God wants you to do something extraordinary, it is because He wants to

---

60 Genesis 39:9

do something extraordinary for you. Sowing a radical seed makes you a candidate to receive a hundredfold return. The power is not in the seed; the power is in the obedience.

I have always had a mental picture of what the future held for me and what the future still holds for me. I am neither talking about my ambitions nor the goals I want to accomplish over the next few years but, as Bishop David Oyedepo[61] rightly stated, "A future as gleaned from the word of God."[62] I am talking about the kind of future that God described in many places in the Bible.[63] You cannot see a vision of such a future and not believe! You cannot see such a future and not celebrate it! You know why I was so sure about tomorrow; it is because I know that the principles I used to get where I am today always work to my good. There is nothing magical about the knowledge you will acquire through this book; it is a practical engagement of tested and proven principles.

In writing this book, I have shared my true life stories, and the goal is that readers will be inspired to discover something that will work for them. Your vision can only go as far as your passion allows it. If it is bigger than your heart, your hands cannot carry it. Until there is a change within you, there cannot be change around you. Remember, "empowerment to succeed" is our position in redemption, and we are destined to be first among equals. Does it seem to you that you will never make it? Has someone told you that you will never make it, never succeed, or never do anything worthwhile in life? I have good news for you; we can do all things through Christ who strengthens us.[64]

---

[61] Bishop David Oyedepo is the president of Living Faith Ministries Worldwide, also known as Winners Chapel.
[62] Oyedepo, David. *Exploits of Faith*, Dominion Publishing House, 2005.
[63] Jeremiah 29:11, Joshua 1:8, Proverbs 22:29, Psalm 1:1-3, Malachi 3:10-12, Daniel 11:32, Deuteronomy 28:11-13
[64] Philippians 4:13

Every one of us has the same amount of muscles, and the same goes for faith. Jesus said,[65] "Oh ye of little faith," not "oh ye of less faith." The guy that is all built up has built up his muscle; he has exercised his muscles. The same can be said for a man of great faith. When things are not going so well in my life, when it seems that I have lost it, I tell myself, "Boy, you need a workout, a spiritual workout, not another church, not another girlfriend, not another whatever, but a workout to exercise your spiritual senses." It helps me to regain my spiritual edge.

Living by faith and not by sight enables me to live in the center of God's will for my life. It becomes easy to trust God. It becomes easy to praise God and worship him for who He is even when circumstances are not looking good. In difficult times, you praise Him because being a man of faith, you know that "all things work together for them that love God."[66] You trust Him so much that you believe that if it happens, it is God, and if it does not happen, it is also God. The mistake that we all make too often is that we remember what we should forget—the failures, the pains, the hurts—and we forget what we should be remembering (our achievements, successes, breakthroughs, etc.).

I like the Bible story of Paul and Silas.[67] They were imprisoned and set to be killed in due time. And yet they remained joyful. The Bible stated that they sang and were joyful inside the Roman prison. When we read this Bible story, we even turn it into a song: Paul and Silas they prayed, they sang, the Holy Ghost came down. We begin to sing and dance, expecting the same results, a visit of the Holy Ghost. It does not work that way. We need to reach a level where we do things for our affection or heart for Him, doing it because we love Him, not for what He will do for us. That is the higher life. Embrace it. Be ready to sacrifice when you need to. Love God and love people.

---

65   Matthew 6:30
66   Romans 8:28
67   Acts 16:19-30

Love yourself well enough for other people to love you and respect you. More and more people have stopped going to church because lots of us Christians are not who we profess to be. We are not examples of Christ. A lot of Christians act like they know it all, but they are not doing any of the life of a true Christian. Personally, I want to live a life that people will see and say, "I want what he has; I want that." It makes it easier to make the right decision when you want people to emulate you, when you treat people the way you like to be treated. Will an unbeliever choose to honor God because of how you live your life? Because of your personal character, their experience of you, can they become believers? Be consistent in showing love to people until you break through their inhibitions. Be patient with them. Love God, love your neighbor as you love yourself, and understand your place in destiny.

I have been mentored by Bishop Oyedepo. I am not the type that fears the enemy, the devil. I do not go to diviners or so called prophets. Mum used to attend the Apostolic Faith Church, where they had prophets who ministered to them about future events. Mum did listen to them every now and then. I always told her not to give updates to me about what they said. To me, they usually prophesy things that are obvious, or they bring disunity to families by providing false prophesies: prophecy on who is after you or who is trying to do you wrong. Being a man of faith, I believe that in this age of grace, God can speak to me directly. I live above principalities and powers. Fortunately, they always prophesied good about me; that I would be great, that I would do well. I kept telling Mum, "You don't need them to tell you all this. Come join us at Living Faith Church. All these prophesies are already in the Bible; God already promised all that to His sons."

I told her my story about my first day at Living Faith Church (a.k.a Winners Chapel); it was not like any Sunday service that I have ever attended. I was not used to the atmosphere, but for some reason, I enjoyed it. It felt like I was where I needed to be, where I ought to be. The people, the message, and the ambience all appealed to me. I went back the next Sunday and the next. I was still a member of Qua Iboe Church then, so I would attend the 7:00 a.m. service at Winners Chapel and then go for the 9:00 a.m. service at my family church. Eventually I stopped going to Qua Iboe Church and joined Winners Chapel. It was my brother who took me to Winners Chapel; I am so glad he did. It was his first time too. He mentioned that he enjoyed the charismatic church he attended at the university where they played musical instruments during praise and worship, unlike our church where musical instruments were forbidden or to an extent not allowed. We only used a piano or organ. We chose to visit Winners Chapel because he had heard the music and saw people dancing as his bus drove past the arena where the church held their Sunday services. He was determined to ensure that I had the experience.

On our first visit, we got there late; the praise and worship session had already passed. Due to our tardiness, we missed our main purpose of being there. I did not know what else to expect. We were welcomed by the hospitality group. Those people could smile; I loved them. They seemed to enjoy what they do, greeting people as they arrived for church. Next we met the ushers at the entrance of the auditorium; another stood at every corner that we had to go through to get to the available seats in the auditorium. They all pointed to available seats. The church was so organized. The ushers had badges that identified them. I had enjoyed the experience so far. After we sat down, the testimony time came. A few people came up to the altar to give their testimonies. Then the pastor came to preach. He was eloquent and forceful in his teaching, like a man who had authority. I was amazed. I had my notebook. I wanted to write down everything the pastor was saying. To me, the service was so alive, so lively. It was meant for me. For the first time in my life, I did not feel sleepy at all as the man of God ministered. I had to be back; I wanted to hear more. And so I did.

I became a member of the church, and later, every member of my family joined. We became a winning family. It was not easy to convince Mum to join. But we kept telling her that everyone at church wanted to meet her. Please come join us, I kept insisting. Mum wanted us to go to find a neutral church, and she would join us. She wanted the whole family to start attending the same church again. My siblings rejected her offer for us to join a neutral church. We were devoted to the Pentecostal ministry. We were richly enjoying our individual ministries at the Living Faith Church. In all my conversations with Mum, I stood for my faith in God without being disrespectful to her.

I knew what Mum needed was reasoning, some form of conversation to make her understand why it had to be Winners Chapel. And that was what I kept doing. I kept having conversations with her. When my testimonies were published in our weekly newsletter, I brought them home to share with Mum. I kept telling her how everyone wanted to meet Excel, Chinanu, and Kelechi's mum until she agreed to visit. She visited a couple of times and became a member. She loved it at Winners Chapel and could not help but wonder what took her so long to join. I am glad we became a winner's family. It is a good thing for families to dwell together in unity.

I am just doing my part to remain in the winning lane of life, and if I do my part, I trust God to do His. He is a faithful God. He never fails. I try to live my life consistently according to His leading. Sometime in the early '90s, our landlord was speaking out in public about my family; he was complaining to my mum about my siblings. He singled me out as someone different. He said there was something about me that makes me stand out. He could not get to me. I stayed away from trouble and did not look to take offense with anyone, not even when people offended me.

He said, "This one has a good report, I cannot touch him! He will go places. I like him. Your children like trouble, except this one," he stated to my mum while pointing at me. After my landlord stated this, I looked at myself and asked, "Why? How could this be? What has this man seen in me that made him say that? It must have been the Christ in me." I was humbled, and it pays to get recognized in public for things you do when no one is watching. Events of that day encouraged me to stay the path; I kept doing my part. I never gave up on God, and He has never given up on me. Even when I failed in my walk with Him, He has always graciously restored my soul. That is why I love to praise and worship Him whenever I have the opportunity. In His presence, there is fullness of joy for me. In His presence, my joy is complete.

Anointing for Success

There came a time when I knew I was serving God in truth and in spirit, and I was so sure that whatever I asked Him He had provided for me. During an anointing service in 1998, as the man of God at the Living Faith Church in Aba, Pastor Steve Joab, anointed us, he asked us to complete the sentence, "I'm anointed to become...!" At that time, my world revolved around becoming the best petroleum engineer in the whole world, and that was exactly what I put in my answer to Pastor Steve Joab's sentence.

So when my uncle requested admission for me into the chemical engineering department and the vice chancellor admitted me into the petroleum engineering department, I knew God had a hand in it. I knew God was answering my prayers. When Dr. Godwin selected me as one of the final year students that he wanted to apply to University of Alaska and aided my relocation to the United States to further my education as a petroleum engineer, I knew God was using men as angels to fulfill the anointing upon my life. When I went to the USA embassy in Lagos, Nigeria, and got my F-1 visa stamped on my passport, I knew that was God answering my prayers. When I applied and got admitted to pursue my PhD in petroleum engineering at the University of Oklahoma with complete funding for my research work, it was God answering my prayers. I knew I was operating in His will and anointing upon my life because there was peace along the way. There was this feeling that if God is for me, who can be against me.

When my research papers got accepted for conference presentations or technical publications in journals, I knew it was God's way of saying, I heard your prayers, and if you continue to do your part, I will do my part and ensure that the anointing upon your life to become a top petroleum engineer becomes a reality. When the paper I co-authored as a professional in the oil and gas sector got published in the *Journal of Petroleum Technology* in November 2012, it was God's way of announcing me to the world. He never fails; what he said He will do He will always do. Just remain in His will. Someone might ask, "What does it take to remain in His will?" I would say love God and love your neighbor as yourself. To trust and love God is to do His will and obey His instructions. To find out what it takes to trust in God or to love God, I encourage you to find a local Bible believing church in your area and begin to attend their worship service and Bible study events.

Being a member of Living Faith Church, I looked forward to our annual gathering of believers at Canaan Land in Ota, Ogun State, Nigeria. Members are usually encouraged to make a list of their expectations, things they want God to do in their life. As the saying goes, your expectations shall never be caught short. Looking back at what my Shiloh expectations have consistently been over the years, I always used the prayer of Jabez to make a list of my expectations, which in the King James Version of the Bible says: "Oh that Thou wouldest bless me indeed, and enlarge my coast, and that Thine hand might be with me, and that Thou wouldest keep me from evil, that it may not grieve me."[68]

Indeed, God had answered me and granted me my request. It is amazing how God answers prayers. I graduated as the best student for my department in college and later got a full scholarship to complete my MS and PhD degrees in the United States. If that is

---

68 1 Chronicles 4:9–10

not God enlarging my coast, I do not know what is. In it all, God has consistently kept me from evil, blessed me beyond measure, and satisfied most of my needs. I say most because there is one area that I have always prayed about, and I believe He is not coming late, but He is planning to come big. I refuse to be down about it because I know that He will favor me to locate my life partner, a virtuous woman, whose price is far above rubies and who will do me good and not evil all the days of her life, a lady who will be my wife for the rest of her life and help me fulfill my life purpose as I help her fulfill hers. He has already promised, and I have no doubt in my heart that He will do it.

I think of my experience on August 26, 2012, on a flight from Denver, Colorado, to Houston, 36,000 feet up in the sky. I was reading Kenneth Hagin's book, *Plans Purposes & Pursuits*. I realized a lot. You can achieve so much more in five minutes working in God's plan than you will achieve in five years working with your own plan. When we pursue God's purpose rather than our own, the Holy Spirit is free to move in our midst. He can accomplish more in five minutes than we could accomplish in five years. I rededicated my life to God and became committed to finding out what God wanted me to do. I was willing to pay the price to go further with God.

Winners Campus Fellowship

When I thought of how I was able to make it through FUTO as a Christian, I really did not pay much attention to the impact of my participation in campus fellowships until a Facebook chat with a beloved friend took me back down memory lane. In this day and age, where we all have the ability to instantly broadcast or say whatever without ramifications on the Internet, Chichi was someone who impressed me with her Facebook notes and postings. It showed her love for God, that God is in the details of who she is and who she will become. I applauded her for such wisdom. When I asked about her participation in campus fellowships, she stated how grateful to God she was for being a member. She went ahead to mention how she had a good spiritual foundation from the campus fellowship she attended and that many great men have emerged from the fellowship.

Wow! That was an eye opener for me. I definitely had the same experience. I was deeply involved in campus fellowship activities, serving as a leader in various capacities. She inspired me to view my involvement with campus fellowship in a different light. For some reason, I had a similar conversation with Bishop Abia and Kingsley, CASORite colleagues who live in Houston, Texas, about the great men that God had raised through campus fellowships. I was amazed to hear the heights God had taken each of us to. Indeed, it pays to serve God.

As a student at Federal University of Technology Owerri, I was a very active member of Winners Campus Fellowship (WCF), the campus arm of Living Faith Church in Nigeria. It was in my third year at FUTO that a group of us came together to begin the WCF activities on campus. It was a great experience; I always looked forward to Christian activities on campus. Prior to WCF, I was a member of the Christ Ambassadors Students Out-Reach (CASOR) for my first two years in FUTO. CASORites are good people, and I had a lot of friends there. I was a member of the Jubilee generation, a group of Christians who made an impact on campus. Both CASOR and WCF were fellowships where good things never ceased, and I am so grateful to God for being a member. I had a good spiritual foundation attending these fellowship programs on campus. It honed my leadership skills as I had an opportunity to lead programs and serve as a moderator for events. I also served as a resident hall pastor for one of the male hostels in my sophomore year in college. Many great men have emerged from campus fellowships. I stand to be counted amongst them.

I have encountered Christians who say that their involvement in campus fellowship activities or other leadership positions on campus was the cause of their poor academic performance. Could that be true? I believe the problem could be that these students were not able to balance study time with other engagements. This is a reminder that we all must take time management seriously. Before I got into the university, I heard stories of Christians who were very busy in the house of God but ended as failures in their academics.

These were stories my siblings shared with me. This became a burden to me because I was determined to serve God faithfully while on campus. Knowing God as a covenant-keeping God helped assuage this fear. I knew that if I did my part, I could count on God to keep his part. I entered a covenant with God to serve Him while He granted me academic success. In His word, He promised that I shall be a high achiever. I shall be the head and not the tail. I shall obtain good success. This helped me remain focused while carrying out my duties in the fellowship because I knew that God Himself would teach me and my understanding would be great.

Another observation I made was that I utilized my free time effectively. There was no time for playing around, which made people call me an odd person who lived a triangular life—a person who only went to the church, his classrooms, or his dorm room. The truth of the matter is that I was more productive living this way. In my second year, I was nominated for a leadership position in my campus fellowship (CASOR). During the interview, I was asked what positions I would be interested in or where I was being led to serve. I had already thought of the positions that could not affect my study plans. I chose the office of the librarian. They asked me for another position of interest; after a while, I chose the office of the assistant secretary general.

Though I knew that position is usually reserved for ladies, I wanted that position because I saw it as a way of not getting too involved in running the campus fellowship. The way I viewed it, an assistant secretary would not be as busy as the secretary general of the fellowship. The same goes for the office of the librarian; the librarian serves as the custodian for all the study materials and textbooks that have been donated to the fellowship. I would not mind being in charge of those at all. He or she is also required to organize tutorial classes for freshman and sophomore classes in school. It was a way to reach out to students on campus. I wanted that position because I was already involved in teaching tutorial classes, so being the organizer would not add any extra work to my schedule. I had planned it all and thought through it.

As God would have it, I was not elected into any of those positions. It was a bittersweet experience. I was happy I did not have to pass through the stress of being an executive member of the campus fellowship, which would have been stressful. On the other hand, I was bitter because a part of me wanted to serve. Later, I felt I could exempt myself from some duties in the house of God because of the required time commitment. I felt I was in school for academic purposes and chose to keep it that way. I never really purposely stayed away from main fellowship programs, but I stayed away from some meetings in the guise that I was busy with studies. To my uttermost dismay, I realized that I was soon going down the drain, both academically and spiritually. I found myself making a "C" grade in a computer science introductory course, a class where people I had tutored made "A"s. I found some easy courses difficult in the exam hall and could not comprehend some lecture notes. My free time was spent in unfruitful discussions, and sometimes I just felt so tired that I slept in. It became a period of struggle.

I prayed about it; God showed me mercy, and soon I was on a return path to my maker. God will always keep His part of the covenant. It was a lesson indeed because after my return to God, the glory was restored. After this encounter, God began to bring people who had various academic problems my way, and the grace of God was always available to share my thoughts and experience with them. It was around this period that I began to give academic seminars on campus, and I realized I had ways of studying that I could share with people. It was in this same period that God led it in my heart to write this book. Indeed, I owe my life to the grace of God so I can boldly say that, "I am who I am by the grace of God." I am complete in Him. No matter your positions in authority, whether you are the president of your campus fellowship or the student union government, learn to maximize your time. Time management and serving God were essential keys for me.

Chapter **14**

Living My Dream

"A man is not old until regrets take the place of dreams." - John Barrymore[69]

I Had a Dream

It is the possibility of having a dream come true that makes life interesting. You cannot catch a covenant dream without it showing practically in your life. There is a difference between a young man that has a dream he is living for that wakes him up each day, a future that he looks forward to, and someone that has no dream, no big picture of what the future holds. The difference between two men—one with focus and another without focus—is that the one with focus will come out victorious.

I am scared of people who take each day as it comes. I am scared living that way because I know that it brings a lot of depressing

---
69 John Sidney Blyth, better known as John Barrymore, was an American actor of stage and screen.

moments, anger, and distrust. It brings the highs and lows of life. It makes for a life of anguish. You do not know what is next; you just live for today. That is why you see people drink until they are knocked out. They do not want to remember what they did yesterday. They smoke until their lungs rot. I cannot help but wonder if someone was about to pick up the first cigarette of his life and you showed him a picture of the lungs and heart now and in five or ten years' time—what it would look like with or without a smoking habit—would he change his mind about lighting that first cigarette? Think about it, will you?

In the Bible,[70] Joseph was a man who had a clear image of what his future held. It was so clear that he ended up in prison in order to get to this image of his future. Joseph's place in the king's palace was only guaranteed by his visit to the prison. Please understand this; the prison presented an open door to Joseph. He could not have met the butler and the king's cup bearer if he had succumbed to Potiphar's wife and enjoyed what most young men would consider a free moment of pleasure. If you believe in your dreams, like Joseph did, you will have the endurance to stay the course—please have a dream you believe in. Every man should have a dream. I have a dream, a purpose that God wants me to accomplish. One thing that could stop you from fulfilling your destiny and dreams is lack of CHARACTER. Joseph passed his character test, so he was able to live his dreams and fulfill his destiny. If he failed, it would have affected his destiny. Think about it—if Joseph acceded to the pleasure of sleeping with his master's gorgeous wife, would he still be able to receive the revelations that made him the second in command in the land? Certainly, this is a clear case of the fulfillment of God's promise that if you are willing and obedient, you will eat the good of the land.[71]

Friends, there is only one person in the world who could spoil God's plan for your life, and that person is you. If you make the

---

70 Genesis 39
71 Obadiah 1:19

wrong choices, you will fail to fulfill your dreams and your destiny. It is not too late; you could have made some wrong choices, but it is never too late to make amends. Let your dream determine who you belong to. Choose your associates carefully. Any time you tolerate mediocrity in others, it increases your mediocrity. I have found it is better to be alone than in the wrong company. If God gave you the dream, He will make a way for you to accomplish it. Some think that they have ruined their life and certain events have taken them so far away from where they ought to be.

As I get older, I have come to realize God is bigger than we think He is. People are not as big as I think they are; my situations are not as big as I think they are. God was working to use the winds to get me to the Promised Land. When God has given you a dream, He does not ignore what you have been through. Your scars can help you realize your dreams. The deeper your hurts and pains, the more God is going to use you to reach others. This is prevalent in America; you see people who have survived something or been through horrible situations volunteer to reach out to people who are currently going through similar problems. As a student, I always thanked God for the academic breakthroughs he brought my way, and I always looked forward to giving academic seminars. That was my way of giving back to the community: giving lectures and teaching during my vacation. As a boy, I was given opportunities to memorize scriptures and standing at the pulpit during some special occasions, such as the children's harvest in those days. This provided me with an opportunity to grow my brain and learn one or two things about public speaking by standing in front of hundreds to deliver a Bible passage.

Farming taught me another valuable life lesson. Mother always took us to the village during farming season to cultivate crops—usually cassava, melon, maize, yam, and cocoyam. I hated the cultivation part of farming and loved the rewards—the harvest that comes after cultivation. Farming is not as straightforward as you might think; you plant the crops, and after a few weeks, weeds will grow alongside the crops, so you have to come back and weed to remove the unwanted plants so that they are not fighting with your crops for the available nutrients in the ground. I always wondered if it could be possible to develop a chemical to use on the whole farmland that could just destroy the weeds and leave the crops to benefit from the fertilizer that you apply after removing weeds. You know, like a computer program: If crop1 or crop2, go to line 5; if weed1 or weed2 or weed3, destroy; if crop3, go to line 5. Line 5, Add fertilizer to the plant.

Globally, farmers would make you a billionaire if you can invent such a product. They would make you their hero and reward you financially, and you would probably get inducted into one or two halls of fame. Maybe such chemical already exists, like the one used for grass lawns. To me, weeding was the most difficult part of crop cultivation; you have to know which plants are crops and which to destroy as weeds or unwanted plants. Even some crops could be weeds when they are in the wrong farmland, e.g., a cassava crop in a rice farm will be considered a weed. A cocoyam plant in a cassava farmland will be uprooted as a weed. I was never allowed to be excused from what I had to do—go to the farm with my family. Come what may, we had to complete the farm work in a limited time schedule so that we could go back to the city before the school term began.

You see, this was easy for us to do because mother was a teacher, and we all got the same holiday period; it was easy for all of us to be on the same schedule. Farming was a great source of finance for us; every now and then we harvested the produce and sold it at the market to raise money. At times we did not even have our transportation money back to the city, but thanks to our farm produce, all we needed to do was turn cassava to garri (a staple food in Nigeria) and sell it at the market for good money, and we were good to go. This way of generating money taught me valuable lessons as a boy. There are rewards in labor; there is dignity in labor. It is a good way to make money. If you produce what people want, they will pay you for it. I realized the same thing goes with education. If you are well educated, you get employed for your skills and you get paid big money, not for manual labor but for your intellectual ability. Because I did not like farming very much, I realized I needed to put in efforts towards my studies in school, and boy, did I do that.

Against my will and unknowingly to my lifetime credit, I would have that invaluable quality etched deeply and permanently into my childhood character. There is a reward for labor. Seeing farms that are not well kept gives you this view about life. You can see two farms on adjacent plot of land: one that is well-kept and nourished while another looks like it has been abandoned, un-kept, and with weeds as tall as the plants crowding the plants. The owner has not come to remove the weeds. So the weeds are stripping the crops of valuable nutrients. The crops appear malnourished, yellowish in color (lacking chlorophyll), while the well-kept farm appears a deep, luxurious green.

This could be likened to what happens in the life of a believer; when you spend time studying God's word, you are feeding your spirit, and you get nourished. When you starve the flesh and feed your spirit, that is like killing the weeds in the farm so that your spirit is nourished. The same thing applies to students. When you study your materials, do your homework, and ask questions, you become like the farmland that is well kept; your mind will be alert, and you will have answers to the questions thrown at you. But when you come unprepared, play around with boys or girls, and do not pay attention to your books or school work, you allow the weeds to occupy your heart, and you will have no answer to questions that could be thrown at you at the exam hall. It is easy for one to be focused on the wrong things or be lost in thought for all the sweet names that his or her lover calls him or her instead of preparing answers to exam questions. In the exam hall, you can see people with minds like flourishing farmland and students with minds like the farmland with malnourished plants. Choose this day where you belong or where you want to belong. I made my choice a long time ago—the choice of a disciplined life and doing what is required to get that which is desired.

One Big, Happy Family

One big secret of my family's success, to this day, is that we are united. I call it the one big, happy family. Whenever I was away, I always looked forward to coming home because I knew I was coming back to a peaceful home, a home where everyone was willing to sacrifice their comfort for the greater good, a home where every member of the family lived for each other and was determined to sacrifice their individual ambitions and needs to achieve a common goal. As the Bible says, see how good and how pleasant it is for brethren to dwell together in harmony.[72] I say this because I recall several times when there was no food at home, mother's salary had not been paid, and my brother, who was old enough to do manual labor work, would go work on house building projects around our neighborhood and use this money to buy food for the family. Not that he did not have his personal needs to fulfill; he was sacrificing his personal needs for the greater good—family unity.

I recall days when I was teaching in private school before I got admission into the university, and when my siblings would come back from the university, they would need money to return back to school. Mother would be owed three months' salary as a teacher, sometimes up to four, five, even six months' salary; then I would give my salary to my mother to give my siblings so they could return back to school. At times we used profits that we made from hawking goods at the motor park. I recall the first fridge that we possessed; we bought it from the proceeds of one summer's sales. It was a fulfilling experience; I could look at the fridge and call it the rewards for my labor. It felt good to finally use the money that I had generated from sales for something tangible—something one could touch or see around the family every day. It gave us a sense of gratitude and appreciation for the labor we put in.

And it became a source of that inner drive to achieve more and make more profits. Who knows what else you could purchase? And

---

72 Psalm 133:1

make profits we did. Whatever opportunity we had, we used. Even as the best graduating student in my department, I still sold boiled eggs and bread at the motor park during the holidays. It did not diminish who I was; it did not make me a lesser individual. It was a means to an end; a godly means to an end. I would rather work and be rewarded by reaching my goals than sit down and wait for what I needed to be given to me. You see, life does not give you what you want; life wants you to go get it. And if you arise, you will get it. I learned this at an early age through farming; it is what you give to the earth that it returns back to you. If you do not plant, there will be nothing to reap during harvest. Another important decision that we made as a family when we received my late father's gratuity was to buy a plot of land in the city. We later built a three-bedroom single family home and moved into the house in the tail end of the 20th century.

Chapter  15

No More Excuses

The majority of men meet with failure because of their lack of persistence in creating new plans to take the place of those which fail. - Napoleon Hill[73]

Seek opportunities to turn your problems into solutions, and stay away from giving excuses. Find your areas of strength, and be the best in them. This will help you overcome low self-esteem. Find an area where you can be the best. Developing healthy self-esteem will help you in every area of life. Also, identify your areas of weakness, and do something about them. I recall when I joined the drama team, as I used to be really shy. I remember my colleagues calling me a dummy. Yeah, I heard them, but I did not let that stop me. The very first time I participated in a live drama sketch at Living Faith Church (Winners Chapel), Aba, a church with more than 2,000 members in

---

73 Hill, Napoleon. *Think and Grow Rich*. Tarcher; Revised Exp edition (August 18, 2005)

attendance each Sunday back in early 2000s, I tell you the truth, the walk from the back to the pulpit was one of the longest 50m walks of my life. The pulpit is centrally located in a huge church auditorium, so I had to walk down an aisle with people sitting on both sides.

To tell you the truth, I did not see anybody's face; I just saw heads and people wearing different colors of clothing. I could not look at anyone's face long enough to establish focus. Thank God I did not trip or fall, I successfully made it to the altar. After I got to the altar and delivered my message, I still remember a part of that message; we were acting a drama that shows what people do after a church service, basically fellowship after fellowship and how to apply your faith. So I was the pastor and I was to come in and give a charge to end the service, more like imitating how our senior pastor usually ends services. My senior pastor then was Pastor Bamigboye, and I loved this saying of his: "I release you as an arrow from the hand of a mighty man; go and hit your target." The first time I heard those words, it ministered to me. So I incorporated it in my closing charge for the drama script, and my leaders loved it, so we rowed with it.

To cut the long story short, that day was successful; people congratulated me for a job well done, but what they did not know was the fight within—the scared boy who could not look at anybody's face long enough to establish focus while presenting the pastoral charge. A boy so scared at times that he wished the world would just come to an end or that he could disappear somehow and be lying in bed at home. I participated in several other drama scripts, and the more I acted, the more the fear went away, until I became a regular. I started writing scripts. It got to a time where I would travel back from college, get into Aba on Saturday, practice with the church drama team, and minister the next day during Sunday service. I led the drama team for my platoon during my National Youth Service Corps (NYSC) camp, and we won a second place award. Joining the drama team helped me overcome the fear of speaking in front of a crowd.

As you cultivate a winning attitude, people are going to call you names. That should not be an excuse; the truth remains, as Pastor Steve Joab once said, "If you refuse to be distracted, your distracters will soon be attracted." I have said it before and I will say it again, doing right is not popular. People called me names. They thought I was living a depressing life, but I kept doing my best and refused to be distracted. Today they are all speaking well of me. They all want to come back and be associated with me. Hard work and discipline pay!

The people calling you names today will be the same people admiring you in five, 10, 15 years' time. Then they will want to be like you. They will want to have your job, drive your type of car, or live in the area of town where you live, but it will be too late because they have not paid the price that you paid to get there. This makes it more important to desist from following the crowd. That is a good reason I refused to follow the crowd; I rather chose to stand out and do what other people would normally not do. It is okay to stand out and be a pacesetter. A wise man once said, in the kingdom you have to be called a fool to be full. In fact, I have been called more. I have been called a ju-man; if you are Nigerian, you will understand that is another way of calling one stupid.

I turned that to Jew man and encouraged myself by saying that Christ, too, was a Jew. So there must be some good about Jew men. I am lucky to be one of them. I try not to see myself as better than others, because I do not know what the future holds for each individual. The person I see on the streets selling boiled eggs or bread today could be a bank manager in a few years. The person you see operating a cassava grinding machine today could be the best graduating student in her or his college in a few months. This was my experience growing up.

Maintain Your Focus

When you are not focused, you go to places you are not supposed to go. Focus is so important if you want to make a success of your life here on earth. Focus determines where you go, the relationships that you honor, and the company that you keep. There are so many people today who are everywhere. Without focus, you will be doing things you should not be doing. Focus prevents you from feeling regretful because you are living a godly life, and you are doing things that bring joy in your heart.

You are focused on doing what you are supposed to be doing, saying things you are supposed to be saying, and going where you are supposed to be going. Live by vision, and have a focus. I tell you, if you fell into a ditch, if you have focus, you will come out. Remember, today is the tomorrow we talked about yesterday. Your future is determined by the decisions you make today. As you go on in life, there are many things that will want or try to break your focus: friends or so called friends, people that do not share the vision you carry, and those that do not understand the passion you carry and where you are going in your life. These are people that do not carry the fire you carry; people that do not believe in your dreams; people that do not want your success. Friends, the absence of focus could affect you even in the normal events of life.

Think of accidents that happen on the roads; most of them are due to the absence of focus. Take your eye of the road for a second, and anything can happen. Today a lot of cities in the USA have laws that forbid talking on the phone or the dreaded texting and driving because of the number of accidents that are caused by people using phones. Think of what happens when a driver nods off while driving during a long distance journey. There are several companies that limit their drivers from driving for more than four hours without a break or driving for more than a total of eight hours a day. Eating and driving can take away your focus and lead to a fatal accident as well.

Just like on some roads, when you miss your turn, it is difficult to get back on track; the same happens with focus. When you lose focus, it makes your journey longer. It is not that easy to make it back on track. Your focus determines what results comes your way. You are not down because there is no place at the top, You are down because you are not doing what it takes to get there. I belong to the top; I chose to get there, and I got there. There is a place for you, and there are demands to get there. When you do not know where you are going, everywhere you get to looks like it. Lack of dedication to a cause is the greatest source of frustration in life. Manage what you have. You do not grow big to manage well; you manage well to grow big.

Nobody grows into a business star without commitment to sound budgeting. You can never become a champion when you keep dodging challenges. It will not be easy, but then successful people do not look for easy—they find a way to make what others call impossible possible. They find possibilities in other people's impossibilities. The easy life is not the way to go here. I will quote the lead actress from the movie *Soul Surfer*.[74] When her dad told her that surfing was not going to be easy, she replied, "I'm not looking for easy; I'm looking for possible," and she became a champion in the long run. Look and see the amount of work she put in to get to be a champion surfer. You can do the same; that is how champions think.

Hear Pastor Toye Ademola:[75] "What champions do daily is what non-champions do occasionally." If you want to become a champion, discover what it takes to become one and get focused doing it. Shortly after the summer 2012 Olympics, during an interview with *Access Hollywood's* live crew[76], Missy Franklin stated that swimming has taught her a lot about hard work, so she tries to apply that to education as well, and it has been great. "It feels good to work hard and get good grades and run to Papa when you get home," she stated. That is focus. According to Ben Stein: "The indispensable first step to getting the things you want out of life is this: decide what you

---

74 *Soul Surfer* is a 2011 American biopic drama film directed by Sean McNamara. It is a film adaptation of the 2004 autobiography *Soul Surfer: A True Story of Faith, Family, and Fighting to Get Back on the Board* by Bethany Hamilton about her life as a surfer after a horrific shark attack and her recovery.
75 Toye Ademola is the presiding pastor of Dominion International Center, a dynamic, fast growing, and multicultural church in Houston, Texas.
76 Access Hollywood's live crew interview with Missy Franklin, "Olympian Missy Franklin Talks Life After London." August 24, 2012. http://watch.accesshollywood.com/video/olympian-missy-franklin-talks-life-after-london/1802878330001

want."[77] This decision will lead you to take action towards bringing your dreams into the visible world.

Keep Good Company

The picture you have of you will determine how long you will allow others to torment you. Your attitude decides who pursues you, who follows you, and who loves you. Every man has a king and a fool in him; the one you talk to responds to you. How do you know the queen for you, the one that speaks to the king in you? Mike Murdock once said, "Your best friend is one who talks to the king in you when the fool is acting up." I like to surround myself with good friends; people who see what I see and who will push me to accomplish what I have set forth to achieve. I refused to move with people who were not talking what I was talking. I am the type who lets my dreams determine who I belong to. I take my commitments too seriously to spread them around loosely. You need people who speak what you speak and who see what you see; people who will see your vision and push you towards achieving it.

One vision that I used to weed out a number of people who did not believe in me was the process of writing this book. I got different reactions from people when I told them I was writing a book. Some laughed when I told them it was going to mostly be around my story. But I have had some inspiring life adventures, and I want to be an inspiration to our youth and tell them that if I can do it, they can too. I want to tell my story, and I want people to be blessed when they read it. Some people laughed and asked me not to bother sharing my boring life with the world. Some not only encouraged me to get the book done but inquired about my progress every now and then; those I will call true friends.

I used my visions and goals in life to choose my friends. I have work friends, people I relate with on work issues. I have church

---

[77] As quoted in Out of the Blue: Delight Comes Into Our Lives (1996) by Mark Victor Hansen, Barbara Nichols, and Patty Hansen, p. 85

friends, people who help me maintain my focus on the kingdom. I have community friends, people I hang out with every now and then to maintain a balanced social lifestyle. I believe that my next level requires the best of friends. I always acted on the need to shut the door against anyone who does not contribute to my vision.

I will always tell friends that there is no need for me to hang around any lady if I know that she is not the right person for me. There is no hanging around until the right person shows up. You are better off having nobody than having the wrong friends. Get some good influences in your life. Get away from the friends who keep you in the pit all the time. You may not want to hurt them, but do it in a way that no one gets hurt. When you try to go through doors that God has not opened, you get into trouble.

Assessing Public Opinion

Do you know what makes our road smooth no matter what troubles life may bring or the challenges that come with living? It is travelling the pathway together and walking side by side with a friend—Someone you trust, someone you never need to pretend with, someone who helps you know yourself, and someone you wish is always there. If you are in a relationship and your significant other respects other people's opinion more than yours, that is not a good sign. It gets worse if he/she insists on sticking to his/her friends' suggestions. To me, he/she does not have a mind of his/her own and that is not a position you want in a friend. If you cannot get him/her to understand this, save yourself the imminent heartbreak that is on the way.

Do not get me wrong. There is nothing wrong with seeking advice from people you respect, but that should only be a way to see things from other people's perspectives, and the utmost care should be taken on how you interpret and present it. Also, another problem with that is that the people will only be advising you with limited data—just what you told them. People can easily jump to conclusions and advise you on what to do, but have you told them the real truth and everything that needs to be known before a wise decision can be made? You can try and justify your actions by conducting opinion pools to know how people feel about the state of your mind or what you should do, but do they really know the actions that got you into your current state of mind?

Learn from the Best

I try to learn from everyone. From one, I may learn what not to do, while from another, I learn what to do. Learn from the mistakes of others and the correct decisions of others. You can never live long enough to make all the mistakes yourself. The person who is afraid of asking is ashamed of learning. Only hungry minds can grow. I agree with Mr. W. Fussellman[78] that "Today a reader, tomorrow a leader." I have learned a lot from other successful individuals, my mentors, senior colleagues, and friends. From some, I have learned how to pattern my resume for success; from others, I have learned how to be successful at interviews; from others, I have learned how to be more productive at work. I try not to do it all by myself and learn only from my experience. That is the hard way.

I try not to recreate the wheel if a similar job has been done. For something similar to my current assignment, I will seek out the fellow who did the job before, find out how he did things, what challenges he faced, and how they were resolved. This enables me to not pass through the same hurdles others passed through or make any mistakes that they could have made and resolved along the way. I recall a chat I once had with a friend who took over the research project that I was doing at the University of Oklahoma. Engr. Oladipo was working on computational fluid dynamic simulation research work for Dr. Shah. He called me one day and asked a few questions. He had been running simulations and getting good results, but he did not know

---

78 1926 April, The Library, Volume 2, Number 4, Slogans for a Library, Page 56, Column 2, Newark Public Library, Newark, New Jersey.

how to present his data in a format that I had used in my dissertation. He tried what he could and read the manuals to no avail. But he called me, and in less than 30 minutes on the phone, I was able to put him through the steps he needed to get the results he required.

He was so elated that he had achieved what could have taken him days to figure out with a few minutes of conversation with me. There is a reward in learning from people who have gone ahead of you. It does not mean that they are smarter than you. In fact, most of the people who have mentored me do confess that at my age they did not know as much of the information that I have acquired. It could be through what I have been exposed to or the available technology or growth in general. The fact is they do not have to be smarter than you; it is just that they have passed through the challenge that is in front of you. Tap their brain and get through the results. I chose not to learn only from my own experience. If you try to go it alone, not only will you live a stressful life, but you will be planning an early departure from this part of the universe. Use the help of people around you. Lunchtimes are good opportunities to learn. At work, do not go to lunch alone. Seek out people you want to learn from. Learn from the best, not just the accessible.

No More Excuses

It has been said that if people use as much energy as they use in making excuses in doing their work, they will actually be successful. They will be amazed at what they could achieve. This is the importance of self-discipline, and this is the key to a creative and fulfilled life. Without it, no real success is feasible or can be attained. You might not have the knowledge, but you can have the discipline to learn what is needed and be hardworking enough to work your way through to be a success.

You might ask me, who should read this book? This book is written for ambitious people who are determined to change their life, achieve more in life, and accomplish well above average. It is for those who want to achieve everything that is possible for them in life. To achieve greatly, you must become a different person. The development of self-discipline is the highway that makes everything possible for you. Let me tell you that self-discipline is the key. It is what helps you stay away from excuses. By successfully staying away from excuses, I was able to achieve my goal of attaining my PhD degree and successfully representing my alma mater in the SPE International PetroBowl competition. I hawked goods to raise part of the funds I used to pay my way through school. I refused to allow money or lack of it to be my genuine excuse from achieving my educational and career goals.

Chapter 16

Never Give Up

"A quitter never wins and a winner never quits." - Napoleon Hill[79]

When you worry, you limit God. When you doubt, you limit God. All you need is the boldness to ask; His grace is sufficient for you. God said He will deliver you and never leave nor forsake you. He promised to be your healer if only you can stay the course and trust Him. Trusting God means that you know that if it happens, it is God, and if it does not happen, it is also God. I would like to tell the testimony of a friend who never gave up on his goal of making an "A" in one of his courses in college, even when the odds were against him:

"The first one is with a course I missed the test on due to my tardiness. I and some other students later took the test the same day, in the lecturer's office, under his supervision. A few days later, the

---

79 Hill, Napoleon. Think and Grow Rich. Tarcher; Revised Exp edition (August 18, 2005)

lecturer came into the class and called out the names of all of us who took the test in his office and announced that we'd lost 30 marks because we must have got the information about the test before taking ours. There was no need to beg, as he brought out our tests and tore them into shreds before the entire class. I prayed and asked God for an "A" in that course, which meant I had to get 70 marks (i.e., 100%) in the final exam. I worked hard and did my best in the exam. When I went into the lecturer's office months later to check my grade in that course, he was looking bewildered when he asked me 'Are you Onyebuchi Okereke?' I looked at the sheet he was holding and saw the reason for his question and countenance: Test – 0, Exam – 70, Total – 70, Grade "A." It dawned on me that with God, all things are possible."

Now, he could have given up with a zero mid-term grade…but he ended up with an "A" for an excellent performance in the finals. You can do it; the extra effort is what is needed. This attitude was described by the 42nd President of the United States, Bill Clinton, when he stated and I quote, *"If you live long enough, you'll make mistakes. But if you learn from them, you'll be a better person. It's how you handle adversity, not how it affects you. The main thing is never quit, never quit, never quit."* A stubborn will and resolve never to quit bring success.

I will tell you about a female co-ed soccer player on an opposing team; her name is Anne. During our division three Sunday league game in Houston, her teammates kept telling her to stay close to me; you see, I was the last man in defense for my team. Basically, that made her the top striker, and being new to soccer, she did not really know what to do or where to stay or where to run to when her team had the ball. All her team kept telling her was to follow me or whoever the last defender was and try to go for loose balls to pass to her teammates or kick into the goal. And that was exactly what she kept doing; she kept following me around, and fortunately, my team was playing well, so both of us had a few moments as we waited for the ball to leave their side of the field and come to my end of the field.

"*I don't want to injure anyone or get injured myself,*" Anne said in a low tone as we began conversing with each other.

"*Oh, just don't come too close to me when I'm with the ball, and you will be fine,*" I replied. She smiled, and I added, "*Also, if you have the ball and you see me approaching, just let me have the ball; that way no one gets hurt.*" I smiled as I added that to my statement. She nodded her head in agreement. She was about to respond when her teammate made a long kick that sent the ball our way and led to a chase. I got to the ball before her, and it seemed she did not take my earlier advice. By the time I turned around, she was right there attempting to take the ball from me. Well, she did not; as a matter of fact, she had no chance, as I easily made a pass to my teammate.

Then came another opportunity for us to chat, and as we did, her team began to approach my side of the field. We were under attack, but we had our defense set right. The guy who had the ball made a long kick towards the goal post; our keeper asked everyone to leave the ball for him to make an easy catch, and we did—only for him to fumble the catch. The ball fell out of his hands and rolled towards Anne, my opponent, the novice striker. The cry of her teammates shouting, "Anne, shoot the ball! Shoot the ball, Anne," echoed all through the field. Even the reserved players were shouting. And shoot she did.

She struck the ball into the net with the keeper still on the ground. She was well positioned since she never gave up following me. See what getting well positioned got her? She had no knowledge of soccer. She was afraid of getting injured or getting anyone injured but ended up scoring a crucial goal; in fact, the winning goal, which counted as double (in co-ed league games, a lady's goal counts as double). Indeed, by the words of Vince Lombardi: "Winners never quit and quitters never win." It made me believe that if I keep doing what is right, no matter how long it takes, there is a reward at the end of the tunnel for anyone.

Looking at my life—where I am coming from, where I have been, where I am today—this story is true in the short term as well as in the long run. Twenty years ago, I used to walk the streets to sell boiled groundnut, fried groundnut, boiled eggs, and packaged bread to travelers and residents in the city of Aba to make a living and support my dreams of becoming a petroleum engineering graduate. I could have stayed at home and waited for my parents to provide for me, but I had to help out. I even worked at a factory, Luscana Nigeria Limited, a shoe manufacturer, to earn a living. Today, I have earned a doctor of philosophy in petroleum engineering, and I work in a reputable multinational oil and gas company. I never gave up on life. Rather, I believed in the better future that was possible if I did not give up.

My First Flight

There is a first time for everything. For me, the KLM flight from Lagos to the famous Amsterdam Schiphol Airport on January 15, 2005, was the day I boarded my first aircraft. It was an experience of mixed feelings. At one end, I was scared of "not knowing what is," but I encouraged myself over and over again that when you get there, if you do not like it, you can just come back home. The odds of you having a good life there are good, just like Mrs. Nwadike, a relative who I greatly respect, advised. I was leaving family behind—my mother, siblings, and friends. They did not mind, but I did. Another group that I had to leave behind was Winners Chapel, a place I had been accepted and so welcomed that I always looked forward to being in God's presence there. On the other hand, I was going to a place where a lot of young men will do anything, legal or illegal, to get a visa to enter.

"*America is one of the most difficult places to get a visa to. In fact, they won't give you a visa; I'm very sure of that,*" a telephone booth operator told me after overhearing my conversation with a friend about my planned trip to the United States. He went ahead to tell me of all the people he knew who tried but never got the visa. They have been rejected over and over again. Well, I am different, and you could be too. You just have to go with the right reasons. What he did not know was that I had already received my visa to the United States, and I was going on an all-expense paid study abroad program. In fact, I had been told that I would be earning more than $1,000 a month, enough for me to have something to send home to help out my family. I decided to think of the good and the opportunity that going to Alaska would bring.

The Power of Diligence

One of Thomas Edison's quotes says that many people miss opportunities because those opportunities come covered in overalls and look like a lot of work. This does not describe me at all. I was never the type to bow out because something looked like a lot of work. I like to put in four years of work before expecting my fifth year harvest. Being a person of diligence, not being lazy, and going out to do what needs to be done gets me where I want to be. That is what I do. Most people keep an easy, passive attitude, having the so-called "give me something for nothing" mentality.

It is so easy to be complacent in life, wishing we had something more in our life but not really doing anything about it. We are not taking any steps to achieve those wishes. Well, it is useless to say I wish I had his physique or I wish I had his muscles while you are at home watching movies when he is in the gym working out. We are not actively taking steps towards our goal. He is diligent, but we are being passive. When you are diligent, you do what you feel is right and not just what you feel like doing. When you are diligent, you are determined to keep on keeping on no matter what is coming against you. When you are diligent, you do not get easily discouraged because things are not going the way you wanted. You do not have that weak, hopeless attitude; you do not give up or get discouraged because it is not happening as quickly as you wanted.

No, a diligent person digs his foot in and just keeps pushing forward. Today too many people want things easy, so they fall into the lazy and complacent category. They are wishing for a whole lot, but they are not doing anything about it. I wish my house was clean. I wish I know more scriptures. I wish I had your type of hair. Well, quit wishing and do something about it. You must take some action before you can expect some victories. Maybe you need to go to bed late and wake up early to get the job done. You may have to change your eating habits. You can be diligent in some areas and be passive about other areas. You can be diligent about taking care of your family, doing well in school, and relating with people, but you are not diligent about protecting your mind, feeding your spirit, or keeping your house clean.

Do not get passive when things do not turn out well soon enough. Keep praying and believing even when you feel like giving up. Keep pressing forward and doing the right things even when the right results are not coming your way. Keep fighting the good fight of faith; in due season, the result will appear. Do not let the lazy, passive spirit get to you. Get your zeal back; get your spirit fired up. Keep believing in God's very best for you. When you have done everything you need to do, keep standing strong.

One of the secrets of success is consistency and being diligent 24/7. The first place we lose the battle is in our mind. If you can win the battle of the mind, the battle is already won. When you are diligent, your thought process is about how to get there. What needs to be done to get a breakthrough? It may be difficult now, but if you do the right thing, the results will show later. You might be admiring a seasoned piano player, but what you do not know is the 15 years of training he had to put in to get to where he is today. I recall going for a few piano lessons; I could not put in the effort. I gave up after four lessons. But I learned one thing—it was not for me. You have to understand when it is not for you. I have said it before and I will say it again, when you try to go through doors that God has not opened, you get into trouble. Be disciplined about how you spend your time and the people you spend your time with. Most times we do not bother about the future, but you have to pay the price today to have a better life tomorrow. Do the right thing even when nobody is watching you. When others are goofing off, do the right thing. When it comes to promotion time, you will be promoted. Keep sowing seeds of a disciplined life. Treat even people who do not deserve it well. Do not get weary in doing good things; in due season, you will reap your reward.

As Pastor Joel Osteen preached, every time you treat someone right, even when they do not deserve it, you are making a swing. Keep swinging. One day your breakthrough will come. The result will come at one point, but it is a combination of all the diligent and disciplined swings you have been doing. Do not fall into the trap of being passive and complacent. Stand in faith; just spend more time being right with God. Do not tolerate the "live now" mentality in yourself or the people around you. Diligence involves going beyond where others stop. Your star will only rise in response to your stretching. Knowing where you are going is easy; learning how to get there is the difficult part.

Stop using common sense and expecting great accomplishments. Use of common sense does not guarantee excellence. How would you know what has not been done or what the difficulties are if you do not read? No one excels in anything without spending time and energy in learning. Trust me, I have listened to great men of God and read biographies of many great men, notable among them being Bishop David Oyedepo, Dr. Mike Murdock, Dr. Myles Munroe,[80] John C. Maxwell,[81] and Dr. Ben Carson. Quick successes do not last. Commit to the practical engagement of the tested and proven principles that are reported in this book. If you are not a committed learner, your star is not in view. Nobody is born a giant; everyone starts as a child.

---

80 Dr. Myles Munroe (born (1954-04-20)April 20, 1954) is the president and founder of the Bahamas Faith Ministries International (BFMI)and Myles Munroe International (MMI), a Christian growth and resource center.

81 John Calvin Maxwell (born 1947) is an author, speaker, and pastor who has written more than 60 books, primarily focusing on leadership.

Chapter 17

Nothing Just Happens

"As a Christian and an active member of Winners Chapel Aba in Nigeria, I was introduced to many Kingdom principles. I have applied these Kingdom principles to my life over the years, and by God's grace, I am who and where I am today. Having lost my father prior to my eighth birthday, the future looked gloomy, as I thought of how my mother was going to take care of six children with her marginal salary as a school teacher. Through it all, we trusted God, and He never failed us. I believe the secret of my success lies in my life stories. Hence, I'm committed to working with youths and sharing these experiences and sharing how applying the Kingdom principles helped me through life. With my book, which I aim to be inspirational, I hope to accomplish this ministry."

This was my written response to a class assignment in 2010 that required me to ponder the various experiences I have had in the past and to see how examining and understanding my own experiences would aid me in being the best in whatever ministry God assigns to me. I hope this helps drive home the fact that I love God. I have a heart for God, and you cannot understand and embrace the secret of my success until you realize my heart for God.

In the summer of 2012, I was given an opportunity to minister to teenagers at my church on a course titled Cultivating a Winning Attitude. I welcomed the opportunity with open hands as it aligned with my passion for sharing knowledge and insights that will help people achieve their goals, dreams, and aspirations. It was an opportunity to minister to youths using my life story. While every part of the course content ministered to me, there was a part that touched me as a person and made me look back at my life and reason out what my attitude had been towards cultivating a winning attitude towards God. In retrospect, I realized that by the grace of God, I had made several deposits in His Kingdom that have carried me to today. When things come easy, God is saying, "You have worked with me, and I'm with you, working for your good.

Indeed, as Bishop David Oyedepo stated in one of his teachings, "Commanding God's attention guarantees a change in position." If you think you are doing good all by yourself, wait until you experience the glory of His anointing upon your life. Wait and see the results of the anointing coming upon the natural. If you do what opens Heavens, you will find that God is no respecter of persons. He will open heavens unto you. Show me a man who has fulfilled his place in the covenant, and I will introduce to you the same man as someone who has committed the almighty God to do His part. What you know is what defines and determines where you are now or where you will end up in life. When you know more, you will go higher. It is time to stop celebrating what you know and time to begin to find out about what you do not know. Below I will share some of the Kingdom principles that I have applied and their manifestations in my life.

Say Rightful Words

In relationships with others, what you say and what you do not say are both important. Proper speech is not only saying the right words at the right time, but it is also controlling your desire to say what you should not. Examples of an untamed tongue include gossiping, putting others down, bragging, manipulating, false teaching, exaggerating, complaining, flattering, and lying. Before you speak, ask, "Is what I want to say true? Is it necessary? Is it kind?"

The uncontrolled tongue can do terrible damage. Satan uses the tongue to divide people and put them against one another. Idle and hateful words are damaging because they spread destruction quickly, and no one can stop the results once they are spoken. We dare not be careless with what we say, thinking we can apologize later, because even if we do, the scars remain. A few words spoken in anger can destroy a relationship that took years to build. Before you speak, remember that words are like fire; you can neither control nor reverse the potent damage they can do. The people we hurt most with our uncontrolled mouths are our loved ones.

Be careful when you are complaining about someone's action. As individuals we try to criticize people by interpreting their actions and telling them why they did what they did. You have no idea what they are going through. Do not be a person who talks about people behind their back. Talk to people directly, and start with small steps; let people know how their actions make you feel, and you will have an opportunity to clarify or get feedback from them about their actions. Maybe they just walked out without greeting you because they got bad news and were not in a good mood. It was not because they were mad at you for something you did.

I once invited a friend (I will call her Bethany) to join me for a bowling event. Bethany was a girl I liked and was interested in getting to know better. It so happened that I had also met her sister at a friend's birthday event a couple of years back, but I did not know this. So during the conversation, when I added that it was okay for her to come with her sister, I could tell that her reaction changed. She instantly wanted to get off the phone and call me back later. I wanted to find out what could have caused the mood swing. I was thinking that if I got off the phone immediately, that could be the last time I heard from Bethany. I did not want that to happen. I tried to get to the bottom of the attitude change or mood swing, but I could not put a stick to it. I later found out about her sister and the fact that she knew that I had met her sister before. I had no idea. I only recommended her coming with her sister to make her feel at home. Little did I know what a bad idea that would be. After a couple of unanswered phone calls and one text message, I later got feedback from her that the fact that I knew her sister and never mentioned it made her leery of me.

Wow! That was a big shocker to me. In fact, when her text message came through, I had to open my dictionary to confirm what I thought was the meaning of the word "leery." I could tell from the sound of the word that it had something to do with being suspicious of my actions though. Later, I did get an opportunity to clarify with her, but I learned something from that experience. Do not criticize people by interpreting their actions based on what you know when you do not know what they know. Be open to people and be direct; when you are relating with honest people, it pays.

I recall when a friend acted towards me in a way that seemed absurd. She had helped me pay for a book that I needed for my studies. It was $90. I did not have the money. My account was low on cash, and I was still working on paying off my school fees. I asked her to give me some extra time to pay; I just needed to pay up my fees, I told her. I said this because I knew she did not need the money at that time. That was my interpretation, but I cannot really tell if she needed the money. But I felt she did not by how much she told me she had in her account when she was making the payment for me. One day she threatened to slap me if I did not pay her that day.

This was along the passageway of our graduate school living quarters. People had to come and separate us.

I was shocked, and being my usual self, I retreated and went to my room. When my roommate inquired about what had led to this, I told him my story and in frustration, added, "Why can't everyone be like me?" He laughed and gave me the look. He later stated, "If everyone was to be like you, act like you, then the world would be a boring place." What? He went further to state that our diversity and individual differences are what keeps the world going. At that very moment, I did not understand him. I felt he was using style to call me boring. Looking back, I totally agree with him. I understand where he is coming from. People are different; they will act differently. The fact that someone does not meet your expectations does not mean that she is bad. She may be bad for you but be an angel for another person. You can advise people, but do not try to change them—you can't.

I listen to Joyce Meyer[82] on TV a lot; one time she was speaking on how we should relate to other humans. She started by rightfully stating that "Only God can meet our deepest relational needs." Everyone is born with the need to be loved unconditionally; none of us ever outgrows this need. God did not create us to live by ourselves or depend on people to meet our relational needs. People simply cannot be trusted to meet all our relational needs. As humans, we can sit right beside you and, for a few seconds, forget that you are there. It could be because a pretty girl just walked by or a nice car drove past or what have you. Humans can easily get carried away.

You need to understand that and not expect too much from people. If I am looking to people to make me feel secure, then I am going to live an insecure life. You need to put your security in God—something eternal, not amoral. Do not rely on people to have your needs met. People can help meet your needs of course; God uses people. If I do not trust God to meet my needs, I transfer these needs

---

82 Joyce Meyer is a Charismatic American Christian author and speaker.

to people that I am in a relationship with. Understand that when you try to make someone a god in your life, you are setting them up for failure.

You become wrongly co-dependent on each other. Life has taught me that friends or people can only meet my secondary needs; hence, I let God meet my primary needs. In relationships, do not force your partner into doing what you want; rely on God's grace to help you deliver your message to your partner. Confrontations are healthy in relationships when done wisely. You are not going to get out of something what you are not willing to put into it. I take my commitment too seriously to spread it around loosely. Real friendship is a commitment. I cannot do that with everybody. It means I will return your call, I will be there for you when you need me, and it is more than being a nice person. Tyler Perry,[83] a popular American actor, director, and producer, during an interview with CNN's Piers Morgan, was asked about what he looks for in a woman—who his ideal woman would be—and he proceeded to give an answer that resonated with me.

Here was his response: "As for me personally, I like intelligent and strong-minded women that carry themselves with an aura of class. I like them to be family-oriented, goal-oriented, and open-minded enough to understand just what makes me tick as a person so that she can truly make me happy. Looks can be deceiving, so I don't gamble on looks, but I would be lying if I said I didn't want someone with beauty and brains. Hell, who doesn't? But if I had to choose, I would pick brains over beauty all day because, in the long run, nobody wants a woman as dumb as a box of rocks—unless they have no plans on being with her long term. A real man is looking for a companion in life that is more than just a pawn on a chess board. He wants his queen and a woman who will be his backbone. Every strong man needs a strong woman or the picture is just not complete."

---

[83] Tyler Perry is an American actor, director, screenwriter, playwright, producer, author, and songwriter, specializing in the gospel genre.

To that, I will not remove anything, but I will add someone who has the fear of God in her, because I want her to base her decisions on her love for God and not just her love for me. Being human, you cannot tell who can offend you. What do you do then, when you feel unloved by your partner? Just meeting and conversing with someone, no matter how attractive I find the person, might be enough for me to make a decision if the person is right for me. Later, I found out that I was making this decision based on our individual differences, differences in our backgrounds, and how the individual compares to what I consider my ideal partner. Sometimes, though, I did go too far in what I consider, now, the wrong direction because the relationship never materialized. When this happens, I always search within myself to find out, on these occasions, why I have gone way too far in the wrong direction.

Did I miss the promptings of His leading? Did I really hear God, or was I going by my emotions or trying to fit into the crowd, doing what others were doing? Always, when I cried to God when relationships that appeared destined to succeed hit the rock instead, I would go back to the drawing board to find out where I had gone wrong. And God always had an answer for me. His plans are better for me. I should let Him guide me and lead me to the woman who will be my partner for the rest of my life. He has done so well in every other area of my life, why not in marriage? I have tried to do it my way and failed. I have tried to do it the way friends did and failed. Now I have vowed to return to God; I trust you, Lord. I have chosen to let Him be my guide in this very important area of my life.

Walk in Integrity

The word integrity comes from the root word integer meaning wholeness. A person is said to be walking in integrity when his words, actions, and behavior are consistent with his inner morals and principles. My belief is in the wise popular saying, "The fear of God is to depart from iniquity," and this has helped me through life.

Like God's word said, "It's better to be poor and honest than to be dishonest and rich."[84]

I will use the popular Bible story about Job here, as he was a man of integrity. The devil's charge against him was that he would change and curse God when adversity came upon him. God knew Job's heart and life were consistent. He knew Job had integrity, so He was confident enough to allow Job to be tested by the devil. There are men and women who have accomplished great achievements but did not have the character to support their success. As you aim for the skies, allow God to develop in you a character of honesty, reliability, and dependability.

Become a principled person based on standards from the word of God or whatever values you hold in your heart. Furthermore, remember that although it is possible for you to deceive the world because no man can see your heart, you can never deceive God. If God were to say something about you, could He claim that you had integrity? Your life must be a reflection of your relationship with Christ from the inside out. Let the words you say and the deeds you do correlate with the person you are in Christ. I grew up in a family where if something was missing, we knew that someone untrustworthy had visited our home.

Guard your heart with all diligence. What you let get into your heart could affect how you live your life. Maintain the glow of the spirit in your daily walk with God. The type of books you read will determine the type of miracle that will follow or happen to you. No man or woman is worth you losing your destiny. Avoid the wrong people, and avoid the wrong places. Recognize that you are fallible and flee. Be a Joseph of our times. Sometimes in order to avoid temptations, you may have to give up something to run from temptation. Joseph left his coat behind. He refused to play with fire. Sampson ignored his problem with the wrong women. He landed himself in trouble. He missed his season of grace. It is the little foxes

---

84 Proverbs 28:6

that spoil the barn. Saul was jealous of David's uprising; he could not deal with it, and he lost his place.

There are certain enemies that as long as you remain in the valley, they will keep taunting you. Do you want it bad enough to wake up in the morning and pray about it? Friends, there will always be something that could stop you from becoming who you need to be; it could be anger, jealousy, any fruit of the flesh, you name it. Deal with it. Shake off any kind of mediocrity. You and God are a majority. No challenge is greater than you. It is your season of grace. You are about to see your turnaround. Let God make you and mould you. Falling into temptation is not worth sidetracking from where God wants to take you. You will get there, but know that it requires remaining in the winning lane of life and walking in integrity.

I recall how things use to be for me prior to my relocation to the USA. Things came easy for me. I came to the USA as a born again Christian. I have stayed away from any form of compromise—financial, moral, social, and you name it. I did all that because I loved God. I could leave school for a weekend just to go back to Aba, attend a drama team meeting, and minster in church the next day, all for the love of God. I will say that I was operating then under the anointing of obedience. God granted my request even before I asked Him. I did not need to make any personal request for Him to bless me. He just does, fulfilling His word that if we are willing and obedient, we will eat the fruit of the land. After staying a while in the USA, I was not so involved in the church anymore, and I found myself compromising the values I had come to know as a youth.

It was as if the standards of Christianity in this land were low compared to what I grew up with. I tried to adapt to it, to do what others were doing, and to go where others were going. Before I knew it, things that use to come so easy for me were a struggle to get. At first I did not realize what was going on, but one day after I sat down and took inventory of where I was and the trending of my life, I realized I had fallen. I had derailed myself from the winning lane of life. I cried to God for forgiveness; I lay on the floor of my living room and wept that day and sought God's face. I later decided to leave the big church in the city that I was going to and seek out a small church closer to my house where I could attend mid-week service and join a service arm to begin to serve God again and follow God for a restoration of those years that I had missed out on serving in His kingdom.

It felt as if my favor bank was getting fed again. I began to pray daily, read inspirational books, and wake up early to listen to taped gospel messages by seasoned men of God who I loved to hear teach; men such as Bishop David Oyedepo, Pastor E. A. Adeboye,[85] Dr. Creflo Dollar, Dr. Bill Winston,[86] Pastor Joel Osteen, Dr. Mike Murdock, Bishop T. D. Jakes, etc. To maintain the glow, I gave myself continually to prayer and to the ministry of the word. That was how the New Testament believers were able to sustain the fire in their days. When you stop praying, it is a sign that your spirit man is getting further away from God. To maintain a charismatic Christian life, men and women ought always to pray. Studying God's word and praying helps you become more like Christ, a mature Christian. Friends, if you cannot pray about it, then you probably should not be doing it. I am the type to think before I act. It is just my way of avoiding foolish steps. I am a man of few words, so my words matter to me. I am bound by them. I believe a man should be bound by his words; if you are not willing to carry out your words, then you should not utter them. That is my motto. That is a philosophy I live by. Going forward, I began to set clearly defined goals and targets to be met each day, week, and month.

A good friend, Ndidiamaka, introduced me to the Open Heavens devotional. This happens to be one of the best gifts I have received in

---

[85] Pastor Enoch Adejare Adeboye is a Nigerian pastor and the General Overseer of Redeemed Christian Church of God (RCCG).

[86] Dr. Bill Winston is the founder and pastor of Living Word Christian Center, a multi-cultural, non-denominational church with more than 20,000 members located in Forest Park, Illinois.

my life. I recall her saying that she did not know if I had a devotional that I was using for that year, but she got this one from her trip back to Nigeria. "I like it, and that's what I use. You should try it as well," she wrote on a note that was placed within my gift. I used it and loved it. Since then I have gotten a new one each year. Later I downloaded the "Open Heavens" app on my smart phone when it became available. I prayed over all my plans, and I did not stop there. I worked on not just meeting but always exceeding my set target each time.

I also spent quality time with God daily through Bible study, praise, worship, thanksgiving, and periodic fasting. I adjusted my leisure time. My television viewing hours reduced drastically, and I only watched essential programs and converted the remaining time to productive purposes. I like the wise saying that your TV can make you rich but only when you turn it off. I refocused on God, and God restored to me the joy of my salvation. I was aglow in the spirit again, and unconsciously I would find myself singing melodies in my heart while driving, doing laundry, doing the dishes, or even bathing. Later, I faithfully continued to pay my tithes, joined the Bible study teaching group at my church, and also became a home fellowship leader. To God be the glory.

I began to feel his favor over my life once again. I now have testimonies akin to what I am used to from the days of my serving Him as a teenager. Things began to come easily again. Doors began to open for me again; in my career, at work, in my relationships with people, my health. God raised men as angels to do me good by getting me a job and getting me new positions within my company. To God be the glory, who has restored me to His Kingdom. One of the secrets of success is for a man to be ready when his time comes.

Here is one of my testimonies:

During Divine Encounter Conference 2012, one of my expectations was to scale new heights in my career. After the conference, I felt I could do more at my workplace, so I sought opportunities to move to a new role. We prayed about it at my house fellowship group, and within weeks, God favored me with a role in the most valued asset at my workplace—a position I did not even inquire about. When my team leader was informed about it, he called me for a briefing and inquired if I knew about my new placement. It was news to me. Because I had no idea, I asked him to explain further, and as he did, I couldn't hide the joy. He noticed a smile on my face. He went further to say that his next question was to find out if I wanted to stay at my current position, as I had already discussed a possible petrophysics position with him, but because I was smiling, it seemed like I would like the new posting. "It's an upgrade, I will understand if that's what you want to do," he said. He continued, "We are just at a place where you happen to be among the few that have some experience with the field, and we wanted to keep you for a few more years." It could only have been God's favor to provide me with this.

Secondly, I co-authored and presented a technical paper about my job at a conference in May 2012. In November of the same year, I got a text message from a friend congratulating me on having my conference paper published in the *Journal of Petroleum Technology* (JPT), a journal mailed to all Society of Petroleum Engineers members worldwide. It was unexpected as you do not submit your paper to get published in this journal; your paper gets selected by the editor. I thank God for announcing me to the world.

Notice the Little Things

"One day as I was going into an office building, a man standing nearby opened the door for me. I thanked him and smiled. 'You're the seventh person I've held the door for,' he said, 'and you're the third one to smile and the fourth to thank me.' I thanked him a second time, with a smile on my face. Afterward, I thought how much we take others for granted, even in simple things, such as opening a door for a stranger. We often commend people when they do big things for us, but how often do we appreciate the little things? When a person does something nice for you and you thank them, it builds them up and encourages them. It means a lot to them, just like it did to the man at the office building. Did your bus arrive on time today? If so, did you thank the driver? The last time you ate at a restaurant, did you thank the waiter for filling your coffee cup a second time without being asked?" I was touched after I read the above Facebook status posted by a close friend.

This is the point I want to make: develop an attitude of gratitude toward the people in your life. My prayer is that the Lord will keep you aware so that you will notice the little, helpful things that people do for you. May you not be ungrateful; instead, please thank them and build them up. That is a way to make someone's day. I once got a note from someone who sat beside me at a Joyce Meyer event at the Lakewood Church. I cannot even recall her name, but I just saw the note she gave me at the end of the program as I looked through my old Bible study journal. She stated, "It is nice to see a man, who is not old or married, who is not a pastor, a minister, or something, come to attend to hear God's word. You didn't walk in on the arm of a woman or with three kids following behind you. You came to hear Joyce Meyer, which if you didn't notice, draws a crowd that is majority of females. Just wanted to say something nice because today you have proved me wrong. I used to think that this does not really exist anymore. I know I don't know you and you may not be perfect (neither am I), but be blessed." I was touched by her note; it made my evening.

You see, being in God's presence is my greatest source of joy. There are things in our lives that make us feel good about all the things going on around us. These things can come in a variety of forms. For some people, it is drugs or alcohol. For others, it is sports or exercise. Some people get their fix from video games or their DVD collections. For some guys, it is sex with random girls, attending concerts or night clubs, travelling to exotic places, listening to music, etc. I am talking about that one thing that always manages to lift your spirit and lets you escape the mundane. What could it be for you? What will happen if it stops working? When the booze makes you tired instead of happy, the sex bores you, the video games do not hold your attention, or the music fades or stops moving you? How would you rekindle the old spark? For me, dwelling in God's presence is key. I feel complete in Him, and in the presence of God, there is fullness of joy.

Brainstorm for Breakthrough

I would like to introduce you to the ready, fire, aim approach that has been well established in the business world. Here, you are encouraged to define your problem (ready), come up with as many ideas as you can as fast as you can without criticizing them (fire), then sift, synthesize, and choose (aim). Creativity through brainstorming consists of coming up with many ideas, not just that one great idea. Always look for a second right answer. If at first you do not succeed, take a break. Write down your ideas before you forget them. A wise man once said, "If everyone says you are wrong, you're one step ahead. If everyone laughs at you, you're two steps ahead." Jonas Salk said, "The answer to any problem pre-exists." [87]

We need to ask the right questions to reveal the answer. To find the answer, ask the right question. If you are seeking great ideas, the first step is often asking great questions. The way you look at a problem can dictate how you seek its solution. What? Where? When? How? Why? Who? These are the six universal questions. You do not invent the answers; you reveal them. Find the right questions and you are halfway to your solutions. The world acclaimed philosopher Aristotle made the wise statement that when you ask a dumb question, you get a smart answer. Questions are not meant to be solved from their original perspective. Visualize your problem as solved before solving it.

Charles Thompson, in his famous book titled *What a Great Idea*, stated, "Genius lies in developing complete and perfect freedom

---

[87] A World of Ideas with Bill Moyers, "The Science of Hope with Jonas Salk," PBS Video, 1990.

within a human being. Only then can a person come up with the best ideas."[88] It is crucial to find the time and the freedom to develop your best ideas. I encourage you to be passionate about achieving your goals. A hungry heart is like a parachute; when you pull on it, it opens up and saves you. You cannot deliver the goods if your heart is heavier than the load. There is a direct correlation between our passion and our potential. You could be the light of the world, but no one will know it unless the switch is turned on. It is your responsibility to act out your glorious destiny. Follow what the book of Ecclesiastics says: "Whatever your hand finds to do, do it with all your might."[89] James Allen said, "You will become as small as your controlling desire; as great as your dominant aspiration."[90] Bravery resides in every heart, and the time will come when it will be called upon. It takes passion to bring it out.

Different people employ diverse ways to solve technical problems, but for me, after recognizing a problem, I follow up with brainstorming, which includes analyzing available information through the use of appropriate methodology to identify a workable solution. Take, for instance, while working on my MS thesis titled "Economics of GTL Technology for Monetization of Alaska North Slope Natural Gas Reserves." I encountered a big obstacle. After optimizing most of the parameters utilized for the various stages of the process (i.e., syngas generation, FT process, and product upgrading), I had a problem assigning monetary values to those optimized conditions. When I could not get help from any source, I resorted to utilizing Monte Carlo Simulation, a process where I applied appropriate probability distributions to cover the range of the possible values of certain assumptions on the economic model. This enabled me to develop a dynamic model that presented multiple

---

88 Charles "Chic" Thompson. *What a Great Idea*, Harper Perennial (January 2, 1992).
89 Ecclesiastes 9:10
90 James Allen (1864-1912) *As a Man Thinketh,* https://wahiduddin.net/thinketh/chapter_six.htm

scenarios and wonderful technical insights about GTL economics. Finally, I checked my results with industry software and available literature on the subject matter for validation. I will summarize with these clauses: recognize a problem, identify a workable solution, and do something about it.

Make Wise Choices

Life is a series of decisions. Believe it or not, your decisions are going to determine how successful you are in life. There are no drum rolls that go off when you make the most important decisions in your life. Your decisions in life are not predetermined, but the consequences of your decisions are predetermined. Make a decision to always obey what God tells you to do today. He already has tomorrow perfectly in order. You cannot predict what He is going to do, someone might say, why can't God just show us the whole nine yards? God wants us to trust and obey Him with unconditional trust in God to be who He says He is in your life. That is what He requires of us. And you cannot fail when you do that.

When God told Noah to build an ark, it did not make sense. When He asked Joshua to sing and walk around the walls of Jericho, it followed no human scientific knowledge. There will be conflicts in life, family, etc.; in all, just obey God. He will always make a success out of you. If you do not obey Him, it means you do not trust Him with the possible consequences that will follow. How do you feel when your children or younger ones disobey or rebel against you? I may not always have lived my life to prove this, but I chose to be obedient to God at all times. It is a decision I have made; a decision already made for me if I am to attain the glorious future He has for me.

Is there a better way to make a decision in life than to seek the face of the one who made you? If you do not trust God, who can you trust? Obey God, and leave the consequences to Him. He is ever faithful. Getting married is the next big decision that I have to make. I am trusting God, and here is my prayer: "Help me, Lord! Please,

God, lead me to the woman who will be the right wife for my whole life." Thanks for saying amen to that. It is my turn to be with the one I love. I want to marry the one for me. Oh Lord, the wife that will help me fulfill the purpose of God for my life. Life has taught me that if I am in a position to do something good for someone, I should do it. It is a responsibility, not a choice.

One right step can give you a life of intense rejoicing. It is my prayer that by God's grace the last wrong step you took is the last you will ever make in your life. If you listen to discouragements, it will make you feel like life is not worth living. It could lead you into making wrong decisions. Do not make a permanent decision based on a temporary circumstance. I am a result of prayers from my mother, family, and friends. It is God, it is love, and I feel it when I look at myself in the mirror. I feel it when I think of where I am coming from, where I am today, and what the future holds. I base my decisions on prayer. When things do not work out as I have requested in prayers, I go back and seek the face of God to find out why things are the way they are.

In college, I served as the student chapter treasurer of SPE in FUTO for 2001/2002 session. I was not able to campaign for the position because I joined the race a few days before Election Day. An opportunity came up when every candidate was asked to render his or her manifesto. My opponents made wonderful presentations and were duly applauded by their team supporters. I was lost in the crowd because most people had already made up their minds on who was getting their votes before coming to the election. But after delivering my speech, they saw reasons to shift grounds. A few of my opponent's friends later confessed that they actually voted for me. It was easy to make that speech because I made the decision to contest for the right reasons. I knew things were not being done right, and I wanted to be a part of the solution. When our motives are right, we will always make right decisions.

Insightfully Manage Your Time

Everyone, rich or poor, young or old, male or female, smart or dumb, receives 24 hours each day. Time is a commodity that is distributed equally among all. No one can complain of getting less time than his neighbor, work colleague, or friend. That is why life is measured by time—how long you have lived on earth. If you have seen an obituary announcement, you will agree with me that the age of the individual is always listed. That is the stuff life is made of. No one's life is measured by how many houses they own, how many cars they have, or the size of their bank account. It all boils down to time. So use your time wisely, and invest your time. Time invested yields dividends. How do I manage my time? Each day you should have a list of things to accomplish, and there should be no sleep until they are all settled. A wise man once said, and I agree, *"Don't worry about losing money, you can make it back. Worry about wasting time, you can't get it back."* What you do in your spare time could determine how far you go in life. Use your spare time to do things that will align you or take you one more step towards achieving your set goals.

I consider my junior year as the most stressful period I faced during my undergraduate studies. I had a lot of commitments. In addition to holding the student chapter treasurer position for the Society of Petroleum Engineers (SPE), I was appointed as the academic coordinator for Winners Campus Fellowship (a Christian family) on campus. So I was involved with organizing, coordinating, and giving tutorial classes for lower year science courses (MTH 101, 102; PHY 101, 102, etc.) and engineering courses. These tutorial classes attracted hundreds of students, and that number was proportional to the number of students that called for my attention on a daily basis.

Hence, I was operating a very hectic schedule. To crown it all, I was nominated and elected as a group leader for more than 200 members for our industrial studies course design project. We were required to design and construct an industrial mixer, a loud speaker, a tape rewinding set, and I have forgotten the fourth equipment. This position called for a lot of organizational skills and multitasking to get the job done in good time. I developed a good time-management plan, which I followed religiously to ensure that my academics did not suffer from my busy work schedule. I basically turned the pressure into a challenge. A good challenge makes me determined, and determination gives me the energy to meet the challenge. One of the decisions I made to manage my time was to eliminate unproductive or time-wasting activities from my schedule.

I reduced my sleeping time. I realized that sleeping during the day on days that I did not have an early morning class and studying late into the night worked well for me. It reduced distractions as most people are sleeping around that time. I started by filling out my calendar to showcase the must-do activities. This marked the times that were not under my control. I was now able to focus on the times that were under my control. The times that were not under my control were officially scheduled class periods, church, or fellowship programs that I had to attend; scheduled meetings per my leadership role; and what have you. I now had an idea of what time was left as time under my control, and I tried to fit in every other thing within that time.

I made a timetable for which course to study on which day. One thing that worked so well for me was to assign a whole day to a specific course. So if I was scheduled to study ENG 305 on Mondays, every spare moment that I had that day would be spent studying this particular course. Every major course was assigned a particular day, and some courses, depending on the amount of adequate or suitable time allotment required, got two or more days. Some courses that did not require much reading were combined two for one day. So if I was in a class waiting for the lecturer to come, I would be studying the course that I had scheduled for that day. It makes sense to assign courses to study on the same day they are scheduled for classes; that way you reduce the load you have to carry to school. Also, scheduling just one course to study each day reduces the load you have to carry to school if you were to study a class in the morning and a different course in the afternoon. Here are some time management nuggets:

- Time is the only commodity that can be neither bought nor sold. The only thing you can do with time is use it. If you do not use it, you lose it. The same time you wasted could have been used to teach yourself or in some way enable you to improve your life.
- The only time you have is now. Get busy and use it wisely. Use every minute of your day constructively, effectively, and efficiently. Every minute counts. Refuse to be one of those who waste time and then complain because they do not have enough time. Never forget, resting is an effective use of time, but you only rest after you have done some work.
- Today is really the only place you will ever exist. When you get to your future, you will rename it—today. Yesterday is in the tomb. Tomorrow is in the womb. Your life is today!
- If you do not know how to enjoy or live today, you probably will not enjoy many days in your future.
- The saddest summary of life contains three descriptions: could have, might have, and should have.

Enjoy the Company of Brethren

There was a time in my life when I got caught up in a cage created by myself for myself. I was in an invisible cell. It was a big cage. I could go days without my phone ringing. I just went to work and came back home. I did not check up on friends, and no one checked up on me. Every now and then I would call home and speak with Mum and my siblings. It was crazy because I live in America, where people who live that kind of lifestyle are considered dangerous and suicidal. No man born of woman is completely shielded from the adversities of life. Not me, as you can already tell from my life story. I had to go through something to get something. I do not consider going through challenges as a sign that God has forsaken me. I believed God's word that all things are working together for my good. I held my peace. I was different. My challenges drew me to God.

What kept me going was that I had many Christian programs saved on my DVR and I took time to work on this book. I kept switching from TD Jakes to Creflo Dollar, from Joyce Meyer to Joel Osteen, and you name it. I switched from Mike Murdock to Dr. Bill Winston, from Daystar to TBN, from TBN to the Word Network and to other gospel programs and also watched Christian programs on the Internet.

In addition, I watched sports and comedy programs when possible. Sometimes I worked on this book, but TV time was way more than book time. I was living in a trap; I was in my wilderness. I was on a field assignment in Rock Springs, Wyoming. Living there for about a year and not having much to do did not help. Have you ever been trapped? How did you come out? I realized what I was missing after I moved back to Houston in the fall of 2011 and reconnected with some friends who considered me a brother. They became a great addition to my life. I also realized the importance of reaching out to people on a regular basis; it shows that you care. And people usually reciprocated. My phone began to ring again; people called just to check on me and see how I was doing that day. I felt loved having friends that cared. Through this experience, I have learned not to always dwell on people's shortcomings but to recognize their good deeds and thank them for it. This is what we consistently do at work; we always start our meetings with recognitions by recognizing people for a job well done over the past week. We all feel good when our efforts are recognized graciously by people around us—our family, our friends, work colleagues, our bosses, strangers, and even people we do not like.

Closing Words

See the Big Picture

Inside the November 22, 2005, edition of *The Sun Star* published by the University of Alaska Fairbanks (UAF), my portrait as a slick student leader was presented.[91] This came out of an interview I granted to the coordinator of the UAF's leadership program. Here are notes from the publication:

Excel feels that, as a leader, "you need to have the interest of your followers at heart. Dialogue and honesty are essential to achieve a common goal. I believe that communication also plays a very key role. There needs to be a link between the leader and the follower." Finally, Excel claims that being faithful and standing by your word are integral elements of leadership: "When you make a promise you should be able to accomplish it."

---

91 University of Alaska Fairbanks. The Sun Star, Vol. XXV No. 12 (November 22, 2005) *Slick Student Leader*, Pg. 14

Those were my thoughts on good governance in 2005, and they still remain my perspectives on leadership today and as the future unfolds. I see it this way: If the president has the interest of the citizens of his nation at heart, he or she will make decisions, establish programs, and approve budgets that are based on emancipating and enriching the masses rather than making personal and political gains for the leader and his/her cohorts. I hope that leaders who have the interest of their followers at heart shall arise and occupy companies, organizations, cities, states, and the nations. I hope that honesty will be their watch word and that they abide by their promises of good governance and help to make the world a peaceful and conducive place for us all. I also hope that employees in the labor force, contractors for government funded projects, students in institutions of learning, and all citizens of nations (boys and girls, men and women, old and young) can commit to doing better than their best in every aspect of their life to help make the world a better place. This is my dream, and I am counting on your support to help make this dream a reality by consistently doing better than your best.

Receiving a hand-shake from my supervisor, Dr. Shah, at the University of Oklahoma commencement ceremony, May 2010

With Mum, Mrs. E. N. Ogugbue, at the University of Oklahoma commencement ceremony, May 2010

University of Oklahoma PetroBowl winning team 2007

University of Oklahoma PetroBowl winning team 2008

www.ingramcontent.com/pod-product-compliance
Lightning Source LLC
Chambersburg PA
CBHW031347040426
42444CB00005B/220